ELIJAH
THE TISHBITE

CHARACTERS OF THE BIBLE SERIES
BY JIMMY SWAGGART:

Jacob

Great Women of the Bible, New Testament

Great Women of the Bible, Old Testament

Abraham

Noah

David

Paul

Joseph

ELIJAH
THE TISHBITE

JIMMY SWAGGART

JIMMY SWAGGART MINISTRIES
P.O. Box 262550 | Baton Rouge, Louisiana 70826-2550
Website: www.jsm.org | Email: info@jsm.org | Phone: 225.768.7000

ISBN 978-1-941403-21-1

09-128 | COPYRIGHT © 2015 Jimmy Swaggart Ministries®

14 15 16 17 18 19 20 21 22 23 / QG / 10 9 8 7 6 5 4 3 2 1

ELIJAH THE TISHBITE

TABLE OF CONTENTS

ELIJAH
THE TISHBITE

INTRODUCTION

INTRODUCTION

ELIJAH THE TISHBITE

ELIJAH IS MENTIONED some 68 times in the Old Testament and some 30 times in the New Testament. He is not referred to as a writing prophet because of not leaving any books like the ones from Isaiah to Malachi, but he did write four verses (II Chron. 21:12-15).

ONE OF THE GREATEST PROPHETS ...

No prophet has been more vividly described and counterfeited than Elijah. Many and all ages have claimed to be Elijah, the reason being that he is clearly predicted to come back to the earth to help restore Israel. This will take place in the latter half of the great tribulation (Mal. 4:5-6; Rev. 11:3-12).

THE TWO ANOINTED MEN

Elijah is also revealed as one of the two anointed men who now stand before the God of the whole earth, symbolized by two olive trees and two lampstands (Zech. 4:11-14; Rev. 11:3-12). He is the only prophet whom people try to identify with John the Baptist, and the only one whom John imitated in spirit, power, and ministry (Mat. 11:14; Mk. 9:12-13).

Almost nothing is known about Elijah except that he came from Gilead. He simply burst on the scene as a flaming meteor.

LAW AND GRACE

Elijah said to Ahab, *"There shall not be dew nor rain these years, but according unto my word"* (I Ki. 17:1). It seems from the text that God gave Elijah the power to do what he desired. In other words, He gave him liberty of action, and so Elijah resolved to force the nation back to the law by causing them to suffer. Only in glory (Lk. 9:31) did he learn that grace in atonement could accomplish this. It would seem that throughout this man's great ministry, God would make successive efforts to teach him this great truth. However, at the beginning of his ministry, he would resort to law, thereby, as stated, trying to force Israel into submission. He would find then that it didn't work, even as it does not work now. That's the reason the Scripture says, *"For the law was given by Moses, but grace and truth came by Jesus Christ* (this proclaims Christ as the representative law keeper for all humanity, i.e., to all who will believe; the law manifested man [full of wickedness]; the Son manifested God [full of goodness])" (Jn. 1:17).

"O Master, let me walk with Thee
"In lowly paths of service free;
"Tell me Your secret, help me bear
"The strain of toil, the fret of care."

"Help me the slow of heart to move
"By some clear, winning word of love;
"Teach me the wayward feet to stay
"And guide them in the homeward way."

"Teach me Your patience still with Thee
"In closer, dearer company,
"In work that keeps faith sweet and strong,
"In trust that triumphs over wrong."

"In hope that sins as shining ray
"Far down the future's broadening way,
"In peace that only You can give,
"With You, O Master, let me live."

ELIJAH
THE TISHBITE

CHAPTER

1

GRACE AND LAW

GRACE AND LAW

THE NAME *ELIJAH* means *"God is Jehovah."* He is considered one of the greatest prophets and is brought on the scene by the Holy Spirit without fanfare and without introduction.

He declared, *"Before whom I stand, there shall not be dew nor rain these years, but according to my word"* (I Ki. 17:1).

The idolatrous priests of the northern confederation of Israel, no doubt, claimed for Baal dominion over nature and absolute control over the clouds and rain. However, Elijah would portray the fact that it was Jehovah who ordered the elements and not Baal. The impotency of Baal to remove the ban would prove the impotency of their god and their claims.

About 925 B.C., all the tribes — with the exception of Judah and Benjamin — broke away and established the nation that was sometimes called Israel and sometimes called Samaria. About 65 years later, the Prophet Elijah made his debut, sent by the Lord to the northern kingdom of Israel. Israel at that time was governed by wicked Ahab and his more wicked wife, Jezebel. So, Elijah had his work cut out for him, so to speak.

The northern kingdom of Israel did not have one godly king who ever graced the throne. Israel lasted for about 250 years before they were destroyed by the Assyrians. Incidentally, the southern kingdom of Judah existed for about 133 years after the fall of the northern kingdom of Israel. Judah did have some godly kings and some great prophets, such as Isaiah, but Jerusalem and Judah also fell to the Babylonians in about 588 B.C.

Elijah is one of the two personalities who never died, with Enoch being the other. They were both translated that they should not see death. But yet, they will come back to this earth in the coming great tribulation and will minister to Israel for some three and one-half years (Rev. 11:3), with the Antichrist seemingly unable to do anything about them. They will finally be killed at the conclusion of that three and a half years when they will be resurrected and raptured away (Rev. 11:11-13). This will be at the very close of the great tribulation, which will be shortly before the second coming.

WHAT IS GRACE?

Why do we deal with grace at this particular time?

We deal with this tremendous attribute of the love of God simply because Elijah tried his best to force Israel to a place of repentance by the means of law. There are only two places that a person can be, and that is grace or law. Every unbeliever in the world, irrespective as to whom they might be, is functioning under the government of law. Of course, they do not understand such, but that is what is happening. Therefore, they will be judged by law at the great white throne judgment, that is, if they do not give their hearts to Christ. Unfortunately, due to most modern Christians not understanding the grace of God, which has to do with the Cross of Christ, as well, most Christians are functioning under the government of law when they are meant to function under the government of grace. More than likely the word *grace* is used in Christendom at least as much, or possibly more than, any other word; however, the truth is, most Christians really do not understand what grace actually is. The stock definition is *"unmerited favor."* That is correct; however, it really doesn't explain the situation.

The grace of God is simply the goodness of God extended to undeserving believers.

God has no more grace today than He did 3,000 years ago. It is the Cross that has made grace available to all, at least to all who will believe.

For the believer to obtain the grace of God in an uninterrupted flow, faith must be registered in the Cross and maintained therein on a constant basis.

If the believer transfers his faith from the Cross of Christ to something else, and it doesn't matter what the something else is, this frustrates the grace of God (Gal. 2:21).

THE BASIS OF LAW

Please allow us the repetition: The sad truth is, almost all of the modern church is operating under the basis of law whether they realize it or not, and virtually none do. This is where the Christian is if his or her faith is not exclusively in Christ and the Cross. Understanding that the Cross is so little preached now and hasn't been preached for many decades, this means that presently the Cross is little understood at all, especially as it refers to sanctification. This means that such believers will automatically be placed by the Lord in a position of law. As well, if a believer is functioning in law, God has to deal with that believer on the basis of law, and that's a position that no one wants to be in.

We must understand that law can never inherit the promise; only grace can inherit the promise. God extends His goodness to us, all superintended by the Holy Spirit, and does so in an uninterrupted flow. However, it is only as our faith is exclusively in Christ and the Cross. Paul dealt with this extensively in Chapters 4 and 5 of the book of Romans.

GOD WILL NOT HELP A BELIEVER TO POSSESS ANYTHING BY MEANS OF LAW

Once grace is properly understood, it then becomes very obvious. As well, it is then understood as to how and why law can never possess the promise.

The law shows man what he is but gives him no power to change the situation. Grace recognizes man for what he is, and upon simple faith in Christ and what Christ did for us at the Cross, the Holy Spirit will then give us all good things, which is the goodness of God. In other words, we function by grace, and we receive everything. We function by law, and we receive nothing but failure.

Man, even with the help of the Holy Spirit, is unable to keep the law; so, that route is hopeless. Whatever is done, the Holy Spirit alone has to do it, and He carries out all that He does by means of the atonement of Christ effected at Calvary's Cross. It remains only for our faith to be in the Cross of Christ, and to be in the Cross of Christ only, and maintained in the Cross of Christ.

So, as it regards law, Elijah could not force Israel into subjection. Such a course was and is impossible! Evidently the Lord had given the prophet control of the weather for a particular period of time, and thus he would withhold the rain for more than three years. It didn't work!

THE HIDING PLACE

Other than withholding the rain, all of what Elijah did was guided by the Word of the Lord, which cannot fail.

Cherith means *"separation."* Even though Elijah was in Israel, which was notoriously wicked at the time, he was separate from its impurity, which the Lord intended. As believers, we are to be in the world but not of the world.

As the Lord had and has total control over the elements, as well, He had and has total control over the fowls of the heavens, which He has created. In fact, He has control over everything. When we tap into His resources, we are tapping into an unlimited supply. In fact, to deny what the Lord did with the raven is to deny the fact that God has total control over His creation.

As to exactly how long the prophet dwelt by the brook Cherith, we aren't told. It is almost positive, however, that it was more than two years that he dwelt there.

THE WORD OF THE LORD

The Scripture says, *"The word of the LORD came unto him, saying ... hide yourself by the brook Cherith"* (I Ki. 17:2-3). The word *Cherith,* as stated, means *"separation."* So, the Holy Spirit at the outset of Elijah's ministry would hide him for a period of time. The Lord told him, *"I have commanded the ravens to feed you there"* (I Ki. 17:4).

Incidentally, many Christians are like the ravens. They may think of themselves as having little ability, no talent, and of little worth to the kingdom of God; however, without the ravens, Elijah would have starved to death. God used the ravens, and He can use us, as well, no matter our station in life.

Verse 7 of I Kings, Chapter 17, says, *"After awhile, that the brook dried up."* Two lessons are learned from this:

1. Whenever God gets ready for us to move, the brook will dry up.
2. In his determination to force Israel back to Jehovah, the mighty prophet was compelled to watch

the brook daily for many days as it became more and more shallow. Eventually, it dried up, and all because of no rain, thus impressing upon him the terrible suffering of the unhappy people of Israel. Consequently, he was designed to feel the misery that then reigned in Israel.

Was this a part of the lesson of grace that the Lord desired to teach Elijah?

WHO IS GOD AND WHAT IS HE LIKE?

I suppose one could write reams of material as it regards who and what it is thought that God might be; however, what is said in such treatment can only be speculative. There's only one true way that one can give an accurate description of God. That true way is to look at the Lord Jesus Christ. When we learn who Christ was and is and what Christ did and does, then and then only will we truly begin to understand God. Of course, this information regarding Christ is given to us in the four gospels. In essence, one might say that outside of Jesus Christ, one simply cannot understand anything about God. That's the reason that Jesus said to Philip when the disciple asked, *"Lord, show us the Father, and it suffices us."*

"Jesus said unto him, Have I been so long with you, and yet have you not known Me, Philip?" (Jn. 14:8-9).

CHRIST IS EVERYTHING
THAT MAN NEEDS AND MORE!

If one truly understands the Lord Jesus Christ, he will see who God is and what God is. Any believer can understand Jesus if he will only read the four gospels. Understanding that, we must come to the conclusion that there could be nothing any greater and no one any more compassionate, for Christ is everything that man needs and more!

Considering that Elijah was responsible for the terrible drought, he very well could not live among the people, so the Lord had to hide him for all the obvious reasons. In fact, Ahab, and probably all of Israel, knew that Elijah was responsible for the terrible drought. So, it would stand to reason that he was most definitely not the poster boy of Israel.

In all of this, the great question must be asked as to how far that God went in allowing Elijah discretion as it regarded the elements.

THE MANNER OF GOD!

First of all, we must know that everything that God does is right. It's not right simply because He does it, but He does it because, in fact, it is right. However, we must understand that it is God's definition of what is right and what is wrong, and not that of man. Therefore, the Lord would use this occasion to do two things. They are:

1. First and foremost, through all of this, He would attempt to teach Elijah the great precept of grace. As we've already stated, Elijah seemingly wouldn't learn this lesson until he was translated to glory.

2. Israel had sunk to such low levels of depravity that the Lord allowed the prophet to do what he did as it regarded the lack of rain. He wasn't being cruel, even though I think He was very much displeased with Elijah's choice regarding the drought. Still, this was a situation that presented itself as having a problem on both sides of the proverbial fence. Israel desperately needed punishment, and Elijah needed teaching. Regrettably, the lesson didn't work too well in either case.

WHY IS IT SO DIFFICULT FOR MAN TO LEARN?

First of all, we must understand that God does all types of things with us in order to teach us, while at the same time knowing that we will little respond. So, knowing that, why does He do as He does?

God's nature is compassion, love, and long-suffering, which, in effect, are all of the wonderful things that we need. From that particular element of Himself, He works. That's who He is! That's what He is! Knowing that man will reject His proposal of mercy and grace, still, He will offer it anyway. Some few respond favorably, but most don't!

THE GENTILE WOMAN

The woman that we will study in the next few paragraphs was a Gentile, and as we shall see, she was also poverty stricken. Jesus mentioned this incident in Luke, Chapter 4, Verses 25 and 26.

Even though this woman was a Gentile and, therefore, not a part of the covenant of Abraham, it may have been that she had turned her back on the heathen gods that she had previously worshipped and had called on Jehovah, the God of Israel. Irrespective as to where it is or from whom it comes, God will always honor faith. From the request of Elijah, we learn that the Lord was about to test her just as He tests all of us. Please notice that according to Verse 12, the woman subscribed Jehovah to Elijah and not to herself. She had not been serving Jehovah but had previously been serving heathen idols. However, things were about to change. As is obvious, her situation was desperate.

That which Elijah requested of her was her test. What would she do? A great lesson is taught here. The economy of the Lord was about to be introduced to this woman.

The world says, *"Give to me first, and then maybe I'll give something back to you."* However, the Lord says, *"Give to Me first, whatever it is you have and however meager it might be, at least if it represents your best, and then I will give back to you."*

The woman now had a promise before her. Would she believe it and act upon it, or would she reject it? Thank God, she believed the promise and acted accordingly.

IS THE PROMISE REAL TODAY?

To be sure, the promise given by the Holy Spirit through Elijah so long, long ago is just as apropos today as it was then. If you *"seek first the kingdom of God, and His righteousness; then all of these things shall be added unto you"* (Mat. 6:33).

I teach all of our supporters that they are to bless the work of God as the Lord enables them to do so, and then they should expect and anticipate the blessings of God. This applies to all, irrespective as to where they might live, even though they might live halfway around the world, as many do.

Did not the Lord say: *"Prove Me now herewith, says the LORD of Hosts, if I will not open you the windows of heaven, and pour you out a blessing, that there shall not be room enough to receive it"* (Mal. 3:10).

Some would retort by saying, *"But Brother Swaggart, that was under the old law, and the Lord doesn't do that anymore!"*

Who said He doesn't do it anymore? Read these next words very carefully. They can change your life.

Anything and everything the Lord did under law, He will do much, much more under grace. That's why Paul said, *"By how much also He is the mediator of a better covenant, which was established upon better promises"* (Heb. 8:6).

You as a believer should anticipate the blessings of the Lord constantly. He said to prove Him, and that's what you ought to do. To be sure, He will always honor His Word.

HER HOUSE

In I Kings 17:15, *"her house"* refers to her relatives and possibly even her friends. No matter how much meal she took out of the barrel or how much oil was taken from the cruse, as much or more remained. Once again, please allow me to state that this is a law of God that applies even now, at least for those who will dare to believe Him.

Having received a prophet in the name of a prophet, she received a prophet's reward (Mat. 10:41-42).

THUS SAYS THE LORD

The Lord now gave Elijah a new mission. His time at Cherith was over. Incidentally, it is not known exactly where Cherith actually was. Some believe it could have been near the Dead Sea, or in other words, approximately where Joshua crossed the Jordan; however, that is speculation at best. The prophet was now to go to Zarephath, which belonged to Zidon, and dwell there. It is believed that this city was between Tyre and Sidon and actually on the shore of the Mediterranean Sea. This means that the prophet was in the very heart of the dominion of Ethbaal. As stated, this was a Gentile city. For sure, Elijah had no desire to go to this Gentile place, but this is where the Lord said to go.

How so very much we as Christians sometimes limit God, and most of the time, we limit Him because of religion. For instance, Elijah's religion would not have allowed him to be fed by a raven, which was an unclean bird. Now he had to go to Sidon, which was a Gentile city and, as well, forbidden. In all of this, the Lord would attempt to teach Elijah a lesson. It would not be easily learned.

THE LAW OF MOSES

Actually, none of this was against the law of Moses but could be said, even at that early date, *"fence laws."* At any rate, these things were not something that a devout Israelite would be inclined to do, but the Lord had given command to Elijah, and Elijah would obey.

"Thus says the Lord," is getting harder and harder to come by at this present time. However, the Lord, even as He did Elijah, still continues to lead and guide His people, that is, if we are close enough to Him to hear His voice.

LED BY THE LORD PERSONALLY

I believe I can say without fear of contradiction that everything this ministry does, and I speak of Jimmy Swaggart Ministries, is all directed and led by the Lord.

Back in 1972, the Lord told me to go on television. He guided the telecast in every respect. We were one of the first to give altar calls over television, which resulted in untold thousands coming to Christ. We were one of the first, all according to the command of the Lord, to translate the programming from English to different languages, with such programming aired in those respective countries, whatever and wherever they may have been. To my knowledge, we were the very first by television to pray for people to be baptized with the Holy Spirit. Many preachers told us that it wouldn't work, but it did. Actually, thousands were baptized with the Spirit with the evidence of speaking with other tongues (Acts 2:4).

In about the year 2000, the Lord instructed me to once again reinstate our radio ministry, which had actually first begun on January 1, 1969. In favor of television in those days, we had let it drop in about 1980, but now the Lord told me to do it a little differently. Instead of buying time on stations to air a 30-minute program a day, we were to purchase stations and air our programming 24 hours a day, seven days a week.

The Lord further told me that all the programming must come from Family Worship Center. I remember that some of my associates looked at me somewhat peculiarly when I stated to them what we were to do, with their looks implying that it wouldn't work. However, it has worked, and wondrously so! Actually, at the time of this dictation, the ministry owns and operates 76 radio stations. Of course, we give the Lord all the praise and all the glory.

THE REVELATION OF THE CROSS

In 1997, the Lord gave me the great revelation of the Cross, which has revolutionized my life and ministry and, in fact, will revolutionize the life of any individual, no matter who that person might be. To be sure, this message is not for me only but for the entirety of the church. It is, in effect, the meaning of the new covenant. The Lord has instructed me to teach, and continue to teach, this great message until He tells me otherwise. This we are doing over the SonLife Broadcasting Network some 24 hours a day.

THE EXPOSITOR'S STUDY BIBLE

In the late 1980s or the early 1990s, the Lord began to deal with me about developing a study Bible. Thinking it was something out of my own mind, I quickly brushed it aside because I felt that I was woefully inadequate for such a task, and of that I was exactly correct. However, the feeling would not go away. Looking back, I now know that the Lord wanted it done, but it could not be done until the great Message of the Cross was given to me, which it was in 1997.

I think it must have been about 2005 when the Spirit of God began to move upon me heavily as it regarded this project. I had several study Bibles of my own, and some of them were very good, but I was not happy with the way that they were put together. Like one brother wrote me and said, *"Brother Swaggart, in most study Bibles, when I begin to look up the notes that they have on the text, by the time I find it, I've lost my train of thought."* He then went on to say, *"But with the Expositor's Study Bible, the notes are right with the text."*

I had never seen a Bible that was positioned as the Expositor's Study Bible is. The Lord kept dealing with me about the project until I knew it was the Lord and not something out of my mind.

On a particular day while writing one of the commentaries, I began to dissect Scripture and put notes in to, hopefully, make it easier to understand. While I was doing this, the Spirit of God spoke to my heart and said, *"This is the way I want you to do the study Bible."*

THE FIRST DAY

I will never forget that day. As I sat behind my desk, all of a sudden, the strangest feeling came over me. It was as though I was standing before the Lord, and the great holiness of the Lord began to make itself felt in the room. It was a fearful and yet comforting moment.

I sat there for a few minutes saying, *"Lord, I can't do this."* I then added, *"People will guide their lives by what is said here, and I'm not qualified to do this."*

However, the Holy Spirit settled me down, and then I began to dictate the notes, starting with Matthew 1:1.

We published the New Testament first. To be frank, I sought the Lord earnestly as to what the name of the Bible would be, and then even the colors we were to use regarding the text and the notes. I wanted the text to stand out above the notes, and we finally came to the conclusion that the color black would make the text stand out above the notes, which we put in red, and that's the way we desired it.

THE RESPONSE

If I remember correctly, we printed some 20,000 of the Expositor's New Testaments, thinking that would last for at least a year. They were gone in 30 days or less. People began to clamor for the Old Testament, which we began immediately. The Expositor's Study Bible has proven to be one of the best sellers in the world since its development.

If I remember correctly, the year was 2012. The Lord spoke to me, stating that I was to ask the people to help us put these Bibles into the hands of pastors in third world countries, which we immediately set out to do. As I dictate these notes, to date (2014), we have placed into the hands of pastors all over the world some 220,000 of the Expositor's Study Bibles. Incidentally, this study Bible is translated into Spanish, Portuguese, and Russian. I must give credit to Jim Woolsey who oversaw the translation into Spanish and Portuguese. Actually, Jim speaks Spanish fluently and did a masterful job in carrying forth this work. Incidentally, it took about five years for that particular translation to be completed.

Also, I must give credit to Pastor Leanid Biruk who translated the Bible into Russian. Once again, the Lord used our brother greatly.

Let me give you an example as to why the Expositor's Study Bible is such a help to people as they seek to understand the Word.

Sometime ago after the Wednesday night Bible study, a brother stepped up on the platform and introduced himself. He was an attorney from the great state of Oklahoma.

He told me that he had made a special trip to come by Baton Rouge and Family Worship Center to express his appreciation to me as it regarded The Expositor's Study Bible.

He went on to say how that he was not too enamored with me, but someone gave him a copy of the Expositor's Study Bible.

He told me how that most of his law practice concentrated on divorces, which cause all types of problems, as would be obvious. Consequently, the great book of Hosea was very real to him. You could tell that the brother loved the Lord.

He related how he opened the Bible and started reading in Hosea, but he said, *"Brother Swaggart, when I started reading the notes to Hosea 3:2, I changed my mind about you."*

THE WORD OF THE LORD

"So I bought her to me for fifteen pieces of silver, and for an homer of barley, and an half homer of barley (the redemption price of a slave was 30 pieces of silver [Ex. 21:32] and so much barley. Fifteen pieces of silver and so little barley marked the worthlessness of this slave. No one can fully understand the pain and suffering evidenced in the words, 'So I bought her to me for fifteen pieces of silver.' Gomer was now used up, therefore, wanted and desired by no one! One can only guess at the hurt that filled Hosea's heart as he stood before Gomer. She was no doubt dressed in rags and had been

reduced by abuse to less than a slave. She must have reasoned, 'How could he love me after all this?' He did so because about 800 years later, One would hang on a Cross, who had also been sold for 30 pieces of silver, the price of a slave. That One took her place of suffering that she might take His place of glory. And thus it is with us all!)" (Hosea 3:2).

THE SONLIFE BROADCASTING NETWORK

Until the Message of the Cross was understood, the Lord did not push the completion of The Expositor's Study Bible. As well, until the Message of the Cross was understood, He did not open up the network.

Until the Lord moved upon my heart, which He did dramatically so, the idea of a network operating 24 hours a day, seven days a week never crossed my mind. The following is the way that it came about:

Every morning before going to the television studio, I spend time with the Lord in prayer. I don't miss this time because it's very important. As well, when I get home after leaving the office in late afternoon each day, I spend some time with the Lord in prayer. I do not miss these two prayer times each day, except under extenuating circumstances.

It was sometime in the year 2010. I was seated on the floor in prayer, with my back leaning against the couch, when the Lord began to speak to my heart. He said the following to me: *"The Evil One tried to close the door of this ministry in the 1990s, but I kept it open about 10 percent"* (about 10 percent of what it had been in the 1980s). Then the Lord said, *"But I am about to open that door wide."*

I cannot even begin to tell you how I felt. I knew the Lord had spoken to me, but exactly what did He mean?

The next afternoon I was back at prayer again, and the Lord spoke to my heart in the same manner again. He said to me: *"When I spoke to you yesterday, you misunderstood Me. You thought I was speaking only of the placement of the programming.* (I did think that simply because most of the so-called Christian networks wouldn't allow our program to be aired, with them not only rejecting it, but insulting us, as well, which happened many times.) The Lord continued, saying, *"I was speaking of the placement of the programming, but I was also speaking of everything for which you have sought My face these past years."*

We know that the Lord hears us when we pray, but still, for the Lord to have verified it meant a whole lot. At least it did to me.

I sat there on the floor for a period of time thinking, recalling the things for which I had ardently sought His face. Even though the Lord had told us to keep the telecast on the air (it was a one-hour program in those days, plus the 30-minute daily), we had had a problem doing that for the reasons mentioned. So, the following is that for which I had sought the Lord so very much those past years:

- The placement of the television programming.
- The finances.

- Health, strength, and longevity for Frances and me that we might finish this task.
- The moving and operation of the Holy Spirit, for which I have sought the Lord more so than anything else. It was only a few days after that when the door began to open.

THE LORD SPOKE TO ME

We had a meeting at the ministry to discuss a particular situation, with some 10 or 12 people being present. Actually, we were meeting to discuss putting our Bible college courses on the Internet. As we sat there discussing the situation, I knew in my heart that it was coming, but not then. Instead, the Lord began to deal with my heart about television — 24 hours a day, seven days a week. Sometime in the course of the meeting, I made the statement, *"Here is what we're going to do. The Lord has told me to instigate a 24-hour network, broadcasting music and messages entirely from this church and this ministry."* Everyone just looked at me, but they mostly passed it off.

When the meeting ended, everyone filed out except me. I lingered back because I strongly sensed the Holy Spirit. As I sat there, I began to weep, and I felt the Lord speak to my heart and say, *"This is what I want."*

A couple of days later, my secretary happened to be speaking by telephone to some people regarding programming, etc. They said to her, *"You need to see ...,"* and they called the name of a company that places programming on the cables, satellites, etc. We called them immediately, and the next week, they were in my office.

To make the story very short, they said, *"Reverend Swaggart, time on television cables is almost altogether taken up. In other words, it's very difficult to get on, but we will do our best."* That they did, but the Lord began to work as well. A particular shopping network went off the air, which left many cables available across the nation. Immediately, we began to avail ourselves of this opportunity.

THE PROGRAMMING OF A NETWORK

This ministry (Jimmy Swaggart Ministries) is made to order for network television. We have, we think, some of the finest music in the world, which the Lord has given to us. Also, we have Family Worship Center, with three services a week going out constantly, and then the Campmeetings, etc. As stated, it's a combination made to order for network television. It's totally unlike any other so-called Christian network in the world today.

When the Lord said that He was going to open the door wide, He meant exactly what He said.

At the time of this writing, there are 115 million households in America that have television sets. At this time, we are airing 24 hours a day, seven days a week, in 75 million of these homes. We have another couple of million that will be on the air in just a few days.

As well, we are airing in 25 million homes in the United Kingdom (England, Scotland, Northern Ireland, and Wales), some 25 million homes in Germany, with other millions in Italy, Spain, Austria, Belgium, Sweden, the Netherlands, Australia, New Zealand, Russia, plus satellites all over Africa and parts of South America and Central America. As stated, when the Lord said, *"I will open the door wide,"* He meant exactly what He said, and He began to carry out this task immediately.

The message we preach and teach is the Message of the Cross. According to the emails, letters, phone calls, and testimonials that we receive, the Lord is doing great and mighty things. However, please understand, it's just getting started.

There is going to be a move of God in this world, I believe, that's going to result in the greatest harvest of souls that the church has ever seen, known, witnessed, or experienced. I believe the Lord has told me this. As well, hundreds of thousands, if not millions, are also going to be baptized with the Holy Spirit with the evidence of speaking with other tongues.

A DREAM

When I was about 10 years old, I had a dream that I believe was from the Lord. I did not really understand it too well then, but I believe I understand it now.

I dreamed I was standing out in front of our house back in Ferriday, Louisiana. In the dream, I looked to my right, and there was a sphere about the size of a basketball suspended in the air, which I instantly knew was a globe of this planet. I stood there looking at it for a moment, and if I remember the dream correctly, this ball was slowly turning to where I could see the continents.

There appeared a figure standing a few feet from me very close to this sphere. I instantly recognized him as Satan. How I knew this, I don't know, but I did.

He stood there for a few moments looking at the globe intently, and then he looked at me. He said, *"You will not do it; I will stop you."*

That was all he said, and then he turned back and looked at the globe once again. He then turned back to me and said the same thing again, *"You will not do it; I will stop you."*

I now know that he was speaking of world evangelism and the part that God has called us to play in this all-important effort. Yes, Satan has done everything within his power to stop our part in world evangelism, but he did not succeed as he cannot succeed.

By the grace of God, I have seen hundreds of thousands of souls brought to a saving knowledge of Jesus Christ, for which we give the Lord all the praise and all the glory. However, I personally believe that what we are about to see is going to eclipse what we saw in the 1980s. Modern communications has made it all possible.

YOUR INVOLVEMENT

As well, I believe the following: As God has called us for world evangelism, I know with all of my heart that He has called hundreds of thousands, if not millions, of you for the same purpose. I speak of born-again believers all over the world who support us, and who stand with us as it regards this all-important task. Your calling is just as important and just as real as my calling. In fact, I cannot do without you as I cannot do without the Lord.

The Lord has given us at Family Worship Center some of the greatest preachers in the world. I thank God almost daily for both Donnie and Gabriel, whom the Lord is using greatly. As well, the Lord has given us other preachers whom we think here at the ministry are some of the world's best. These are men and women who have the same calling that I have, and who preach the same message. However, in all of this, many, many years ago, the Lord gave me Frances as my wife, without whom we could not do what we're doing. Her wisdom, consecration, dedication to the Lord, and contribution to this work and ministry are beyond compare. So, it's a team that the Lord has put together for one purpose, which, as stated, is world evangelism. It's the Message of the Cross for both sinner and saint, and I believe it is what the Holy Spirit is presently saying to the churches.

THE METHOD OF BEING SUSTAINED

First of all, God's methods aren't our methods. When we think of being sustained by someone, we certainly don't think of a poor widow woman who is starving and, in fact, prepared to die because of starvation. But yet, this is the one chosen by the Lord who would sustain the Prophet Elijah. The Lord said, *"Behold, I have commanded a widow woman there to sustain you"* (I Ki. 17:9).

The Lord told the prophet exactly what to do.

After he knew that this was the one chosen by God, he would first of all ask for *"a little water in a vessel, that I may drink"* (I Ki. 17:10).

There is some evidence in the text that this widow woman knew that Elijah was a prophet. Whether she had ever heard of him is not known. At any rate, she knew that this was not just an ordinary man.

However, there is one thing here that she certainly did not know, and that was what was about to happen to her, her son, and, in fact, her future. At that moment, she could never realize that her whole world was about to change. Her story would be written in the Sacred Writ, which would inspire untold millions down through the ages, and all because of her faith.

In her destitute condition, she could easily have rebuffed the prophet when he asked for water, but she didn't! She hastened to do what he requested. Then, while she was gone to get the water, the Lord whispered to the prophet to say to her, *"Bring me, I pray you, a morsel of bread in your hand"* (I Ki. 17:11).

While Elijah did not know of her destitute condition, at least not at that moment, it is for sure that the Lord did.

WHY DID THE LORD CHOOSE
THIS PARTICULAR WOMAN?

Every evidence is that she was a Gentile, which means that she had no part in the great covenant that God had with Israel. In fact, she was, or at least had been, and idol worshipper and lived in the very heart of idol worship. There is some evidence, however, that she had heard of Jehovah, but she would have had no way of having further knowledge, at least not at that time.

The Scripture is silent concerning this, so we can only conjecture; however, this one thing we do know, God never works capriciously. He always knows exactly what He is doing and has a reason behind everything He does.

This we do know: The one thing that God always honors, irrespective as to whom the person might be, is faith. We have no way of knowing if in her destitute position, this woman had finally determined that her idols could afford her nothing, and she had prayed to Jehovah. Maybe it was only that God knew that she would respond favorably and, therefore, selected her. Whatever the reason, we do know that faith played a great part. Despite her being a Gentile and despite her destitute condition, this woman would evidence faith, even as we shall see. Let it ever be understood, faith is the coin that spends in God's economy and, in fact, the only coin that spends in His economy.

THE GREAT STEP OF FAITH

As the great prophet asked for a morsel of bread, her answer was somewhat revealing. She said, *"As the LORD your God lives, I have not a cake, but a handful of meal in a barrel, and a little oil in a cruse."* She then said, *"I am gathering two sticks, that I may go in and dress it for me and my son, that we may eat it, and die"* (I Ki. 17:12).

If it is to be noticed, she said, *"As the LORD your God lives."* She didn't say, *"My God,"* but rather *"your God."* This further tells us that she was a Gentile. As well, Jesus also stated that she was a Gentile (Lk. 4:25-26).

In response to her answer, the prophet lay out a test of faith for her exactly as the Lord always does. He said unto her, *"Fear not; go and do as you have said: but make me thereof a little cake first, and bring it unto me, and after make for you and for your son"* (I Ki. 17:13).

THE BARREL OF MEAL SHALL NOT WASTE, NEITHER SHALL THE CRUSE OF OIL FAIL

Attached to the request was a gargantuan promise. The great prophet said,

"For thus says the LORD God of Israel" (I Ki. 17:14).

This proclaimed in no uncertain terms that her idols, in fact, all the idols worshipped in this Gentile land, could not perform a miracle and could not do anything. So, by the statement used, the prophet was saying, *"The LORD God of Israel"* can do anything.

Then he said, *"The barrel of meal shall not waste, neither shall the cruse of oil fail, until the day that the* LORD *sends rain upon the earth"* (I Ki. 17:14).

So, there it was, laid out before her.

Would she believe the prophet and do as he requested, or would she rebuke him for asking for her last morsel of bread?

This was truly a step of faith for her. She did not know Jehovah. She did not know His Word. She knew little if anything of His prophet, who was asking her to give him the bread that she and her son were to eat.

THE TEST OF FAITH

God always tests our faith. What will we do? What will our reaction be? I'm afraid that all too often we fail the test.

All this woman had to do was simply believe what the prophet said. Would she believe him, or would she not believe him? What would you have done?

A TEST OF FAITH

Looking at it sensibly, she had nothing to lose. If she kept what little bread she had, refusing to give it to the prophet, it would only last her for one meal, and then she and her son would die of starvation. So, in her heart of hearts, she made the decision to trust what the prophet said without really knowing what it meant.

The Scripture says, *"And she went and did according to the saying of Elijah"* (I Ki. 17:15). In other words, she believed what the man said, irrespective as to how preposterous it surely seemed at that hour.

What did he mean, *"The barrel of meal shall not waste, neither shall the cruse of oil fail?"*

She had no way of knowing exactly what it did mean, but one thing she did know, she couldn't lose by accepting the prophet's proposal. In fact, no believer, or anyone for that matter, can go wrong by believing the Lord and doing what He has said do. It goes the same for you and me today as it did for this widow woman so long, long ago.

No one ever has anything to lose by obeying the Lord. In fact, one simply cannot lose by obeying the Lord. As well, I believe that this great promise given to this widow woman so long ago is still appropriate for us at this present time. I believe the Holy Spirit is saying to you and me, and, in fact, every believer who has ever lived: *"The barrel of meal shall not waste, neither shall the cruse of oil fail."*

God's Word cannot lie. Unless it is specifically meant for a certain person, a certain time, and a certain place, as sometimes it is, then it is appropriate for us to accept that which He gave so long ago and apply it to our own situation presently. God will honor it now just as much as He honored it then.

OBEDIENCE

Once she obeyed, she apparently invited the great prophet to stay with her and her son. This means that her house was evidently large enough to accommodate him.

When it was time for the next meal, she looked in the barrel and the cruse and, lo and behold, even though she had emptied it the day before, there was meal in the barrel and oil in the cruse.

Some have attempted to claim that God supplied the need in various ways, trying to explain away the miraculous appearance and continued supply of the meal and the oil. However, I think the Hebrew text readily proclaims the fact that it happened exactly as the prophet said it would happen. When she took meal out of the barrel and oil out of the cruse, no matter how much, more meal and more oil miraculously took the place of that which had been taken. In fact, this is God's way.

HAMILTON'S LAW

There is a law referred to as *Hamilton's Law,* which states that everything that we make, build, or perfect, at the same time, also registers depletion in some way. In other words, when a house is built, trees are depleted in order to secure the lumber, with sand depleted in order that brick can be made, etc. That is true!

However, with God, there is never any depletion. He does not destroy something in order to build something. He miraculously supplies it, whatever it might be, as He did here.

Furthermore, the Scripture says, *"And she, and he* (Elijah), *and her house* (all her relatives and friends), *did eat many days"* (I Ki. 17:15).

The famine was sore in the land, and, no doubt, word quickly got around that this widow woman had a supply that was unexplainable. She most likely had many guests for breakfast, lunch, and dinner. However, it didn't matter how many there were, how many sat around the table, or how many partook, the Scripture says, *"And the barrel of meal wasted not, neither did the cruse of oil fail, according to the Word of the LORD, which he spoke by Elijah"* (I Ki. 17:16).

> One wants to shout, *"Hallelujah!"*
> *"What a mighty God we serve,*
> *"Angels bow before Him,*
> *"Heaven and earth adore Him,*
> *"What a mighty God we serve!"*

THE ATTACK BY SATAN

"And he stretched himself upon the child three times, and cried unto the LORD, and said, O LORD my God, I pray thee, let this child's soul come into him again." (I Ki. 17:21).

Whenever the Lord moves mightily as He did here (with the meal and the oil), Satan will then attack. This means that the second trial of faith is oftentimes harder than the first trial. However, please remember, all of it, irrespective of the course it might take, is, as previously stated, a test of our faith.

We find that the little boy of the widow woman died. Elijah laid the corpse upon his own bed. Why did the prophet

CHAPTER ONE **GRACE AND LAW** | **35**

take the boy to his own personal room afforded him by the widow? It was done as a token to show that his presence in her house was definitely a blessing and not a curse. In his prayer, Elijah proclaimed the fact that God controls all things, especially life and death.

The request, *"Let this child's soul come into him again,"* proves that the boy was dead.

Verse 21 also says, *"And he stretched himself upon the child three times."*

Why three times?

The Lord evidently told him to do this, for it actually had nothing to do with the miracle that transpired, but was rather to symbolically portray the triune God — God *the Father*, God *the Son*, and God *the Holy Spirit*.

Death had been suspended by and through the barrel of meal and the cruse of oil not failing, and now again, it would be suspended by being miraculously dismissed.

As we shall see, the statement made by the woman as given in Verse 24 of I Kings, Chapter 17, presents a statement of faith far greater than the present miracle. This Gentile woman would exclaim the fact that Israel's God was now her God.

DEATH

Why did the Lord allow the child to get sick and die? This woman had obeyed the Lord in doing exactly what He wanted, but now her child died.

Death is a terrible enemy and is prevalent because of the fall. All must eventually die, but it is so sad to see the young die, which they will at times!

Evidently, this child, who must have been a preteen, was all that the woman had. If she lost him, there was nothing left. One can well imagine how much she loved the little boy.

Now he was dead! By her statements, she seemed to want to blame God, the same One who miraculously supplied the meal and the oil, but she seemed to be fearful of doing that. So, in a sense, she blamed Elijah.

Her question, *"What have I to do with you?"* (I Ki. 17:18), in essence, says, *"Why have you done me this way?"* She then added, *"Oh you man of God."* Even though she could not explain the present situation concerning her son, beyond the shadow of a doubt, she did know that Elijah was a man of God. This means that as something was done about the barrel of meal and the cruse of oil, likewise, something, she believed, could be done for her son.

There is a great lesson to be learned from all of this. God works through men and women, in this case, Elijah. When the man of God is accepted, God, at the same time, is accepted. When the man of God, whomever he might be, is rejected, at the same time, God is rejected. We seem to be slow in learning this great lesson, but to be sure, this woman had accepted Elijah in totality! By taking this severe problem to him, she, in effect, was taking it to the Lord.

YOUR SON LIVES!

Elijah prayed and God answered! Any dead raised by the power of God was to show that the Lord is able to suspend death. Each case was a portent of the coming resurrection.

THE DROUGHT

The time frame of these happenings was the third year of the drought. The New Testament distinctly states that the drought lasted *"three years and six months"* (Lk. 4:25; James 5:17). So, that must have been several months from the time that the Lord spoke to Elijah until he actually did see Ahab, which would total the three and a half years the drought lasted. The famine that was in the land of Samaria due to the drought was also indicative of the spiritual condition. Presently, despite the enumerable churches in America, I'm afraid the true picture is actually far different than appears on the surface. There is presently a famine in the land as it refers to the Word of God.

The *Obadiah* named in I Kings 18:3 is not the same prophet who wrote the book which bears that name. Among other things, the Lord, no doubt, placed Obadiah in this high office in Samaria that he might use him to protect true prophets of the Lord.

Why was Ahab this desperate to find Elijah? The answer is simple. It was Elijah who had stopped the rain, and it was

Elijah alone who could bring back the rain, so Ahab thought (James 5:17-18).

There were two different sets of false prophets listed in Verse 19 of I Kings, Chapter 18, both totaling 850. Four hundred were supported by Jezebel.

THE SPIRITUAL CONDITION OF ISRAEL

The Word of the Lord to Elijah the prophet was, *"Go, show yourself unto Ahab; and I will send rain upon the earth"* (I Ki. 18:1).

From the time that the Lord spoke to Elijah concerning the meeting with Ahab until the time the rain actually came must have been at least several months. The New Testament emphatically states that this drought lasted *"three years and six months"* (Lk. 4:25).

The phrase "many days" sobs with a divine anguish. What untold suffering lies under that little word! How it seems to throb with pity!

The ground was cracked, barren, and dry. Considering there had been no rain in some three years, every leaf on every tree, undoubtedly, was burned to the proverbial crisp. The fountains and streams had long since dried up. No doubt, untold numbers of livestock had died, as well as the wild animals. Food was in terribly short supply because crops could not be grown without the benefit of moisture; therefore, due to a lack of rain, everything had died.

This terrible drought that had been inflicted upon Israel was meant to portray the spirituality of the nation. In other words, what one could see in the physical was exactly what had happened in the spiritual.

Also, from all of this, as it regards an individual, a city, or even a nation, it must be understood that *"as the spiritual, so the prosperity or lack thereof."*

The United States has been greatly blessed by the Lord, actually, more so, possibly one could say, than any nation on the face of the earth. The blessings have probably been greater than any nation has ever experienced in human history, with the exception of Israel in its beginning days. However, America is forsaking God! It is no longer the separation of church and state, which is right in the eyes of God, but rather a separation of God and state. Such a position will ultimately bring about disaster. It may take some decades for it to come, but if Jesus tarries, this spiritual drought will result in an economic drought too! This spiritual drought is despite the fact that the nation is more religious than ever.

Verse 2 of I Kings, Chapter 18, says, *"And there was a sore famine in Samaria."* As well, there is a sore famine of the Word of God in America, Canada, and even in most of the world.

A FAMINE OF THE WORD OF GOD

Almost all of the time down through history, the Lord has had a people, whomever they may have been, who held up His name and did their best to stay true to His Word. In this great nation of America, some 200 years ago, these people were the Baptists and the Methodists, and especially the Methodists. In fact, had it not been for the Methodists and the power of God that was evidenced in their midst, there is a good possibility that there would be no United States of America today.

However, gradually, these denominations began to lose their way, with the Lord then raising up the Holiness people, who hungered and thirsted after righteousness, and who left a mark upon this world. In other words, they were the ones who were taking up the banner. This was in the late 1800s.

Regrettably and sadly, the holiness group ultimately went into legalism and self-righteousness, which basically destroyed their spiritual effectiveness. To take their place, the Lord raised up the Pentecostals, which was done at about the turn of the 20th century.

Though ridiculed, lampooned, and laughed at, still, God took the weak things of the world and confounded the mighty. They (we) touched the world with the greatest message that it had ever known: Jesus saves, Jesus baptizes with the Holy Spirit, Jesus heals, and Jesus is coming again.

However, today the Pentecostals are losing their way because they're leaving the very thing that made them great, and I speak of the mighty baptism with the Holy Spirit. The cry of the prophet continues to come down through the ages, and it is as valid now as it ever was, *"This is the Word of the* LORD *unto Zerubbabel* (actually, to the entirety of the church), *saying, Not by might* (human might), *nor by power* (human power), *but by My Spirit, says the* LORD *of Hosts"* (Zech. 4:6).

THE METHOD

The method of God's work being accomplished in the world is by the power of the Holy Spirit. Everything that has ever been done on this earth as it regards the Godhead has been done by the Holy Spirit, with the exception of Christ and His crucifixion. However, the Holy Spirit even superintended that from beginning to end (Lk. 4:18-19).

If it is claimed to be for the Lord, whatever is being done must be done by the moving, operation, power, and person of the Holy Spirit through believers. Otherwise, it will not be recognized by God. In fact, it will be constituted as a work of the flesh (Rom. 8:1).

The phrase from Verse 6 of Zechariah, Chapter 4, that states, *"says the* LORD *of Hosts,"* also presents God's supreme power over everything in the material and spiritual universe. All are organized under His command. As well, the word hosts, as used here, is associated with warfare and relates to the word armies. In other words, He is the *"Lord of armies."*

As stated, regrettably and sadly, the Pentecostals are presently losing their way, so who will take their place?

THE MESSAGE OF THE CROSS

As to exactly which *who* it will be, and *what* God is presently doing, I cannot answer, for He is never without a witness. However, I believe I can answer regarding the message that the Lord will use and, in fact, is already beginning to use, as it regards taking the church to higher heights and deeper depths than it has previously known. Of course, I speak of those who truly love the Lord. That message is the Message of the Cross.

Paul said: *"The preaching* (Word) *of the Cross is to them who perish foolishness; but unto us who are saved it is the power of God"* (I Cor. 1:18).

The Greek word translated *preaching* in this verse is *logos*. It means in brief, *"word or message."* So, what Paul actually said was far greater than the art of preaching. It really has to do with the entire embodiment of the message, which is the full message and the total message proclaiming the new covenant, which is the Message of the Cross.

THE MEANING OF THE NEW COVENANT

Let me say it again. The Message of the Cross is not merely an addendum. It is not merely an option, but rather it is actually the meaning of the entirety of the new covenant. I think one can say and not be scripturally wrong that it is an embodiment of the entirety of the Bible. In fact, as already stated elsewhere in this volume, the story of the Bible is the story of Jesus

Christ and Him crucified. So, the Lord, I believe, is trying to pull the church back to the Cross. As well, He is giving us a greater understanding of the Cross, which also deals with the Holy Spirit, than the church has ever known. It's not something new; it's that which was originally given to the Apostle Paul, but the Holy Spirit is now bringing it back in a greater way than ever. Sadly, this is because the church, for all practical purposes, has rejected the Cross. Let it be understood that when one rejects the Cross, one has rejected the very plan of God for the human race. Let it also be understood that one cannot embrace the Cross of Christ and at the same time embrace other things as it regards salvation and victory. The Cross alone is the answer and the solution. There is no other!

THE ONLY ANSWER IS THE CROSS

If, in fact, the spiritual condition of this nation presently is similar to that of Israel of old, or is quickly becoming so, then our economic and political power, as well as military strength, will soon begin to diminish, as well. This, in fact, has already begun.

So, in essence, the Message of the Cross is the only thing standing between the church and total apostasy. As well, the Message of the Cross is the only thing standing between this nation and total economic and political ruin. In fact, the same could be said for the entirety of the world, but it is especially true concerning America and Canada. Now, think about what I've just stated!

If that is correct, and I have no doubt that it is, then it's imperative that this message be proclaimed throughout the entirety of the world, and in no uncertain terms. Its voice must not be silenced, its impact must be felt, and its way must be known simply because it is the Word of God, and the Word of God alone!

"My hope is built on nothing less,
"Than Jesus' blood and righteousness;
"I dare not trust the sweetest frame,
"But wholly lean on Jesus' name."

"When darkness veils His lovely face,
"I rest on His unchanging grace;
"In every high and stormy gale,
"My anchor holds within the veil."

"His oath, His covenant, His blood,
"Support me in the whelming flood;
"When all around my soul gives way,
"He then is all my hope and stay."

"When He shall come with trumpet sound,
"Oh may I then in Him be found:
"Dressed in His righteousness alone,
"Faultless to stand before the throne."

ELIJAH
THE TISHBITE

CHAPTER

2

THE TROUBLER OF ISRAEL

CHAPTER TWO

THE TROUBLER OF ISRAEL

AS PREVIOUSLY STATED, the Obadiah mentioned here is not the same Obadiah who wrote the book in the Bible that bears his name. The latter lived approximately 350 years later.

It is obvious as to the sincerity and consecration of Obadiah. Even though he held a very high office in the state of Israel, he did everything he could to aid and abet the work of God, even at the risk of his own life.

In secret, Obadiah took 100 true prophets of God, who, no doubt, were of the school of the prophets, and hid them in a couple of caves and sustained their lives with bread and water. Undoubtedly, the Lord had this man placed in this position for this very purpose. To be sure, Obadiah did not fail the Lord.

The situation regarding the drought that had brought about famine had become so acute in the northern kingdom, and, no doubt, the surrounding territories, as well, that Ahab appointed Obadiah to go in one direction to look for water while he went in another. Ahab probably had many with him, but Obadiah traveled alone. The Lord set all of this up, for He would have Obadiah meet Elijah. The great prophet then told the governor of the house of Ahab that he should go and tell Ahab, *"Behold, Elijah is here."*

THE APPOINTMENT

As the text proclaims, Obadiah was somewhat fearful of revealing to Ahab that he had met Elijah, considering that Ahab and, in fact, all of Israel, it seems, were looking for the great prophet. Nevertheless, despite the fear, Obadiah obeyed what Elijah told him to do.

As we have briefly alluded, the Lord had Obadiah in that exact place at that exact time for the purpose of saving the prophets of God from death, as well as other situations that are addressed here regarding the meeting with Elijah. How many people does the Lord appoint for things, but those things are never carried out? There's a lack of consecration and a lack of concern on the part of the individual. At any rate, what the Lord had proposed never materialized. Such people are not aware that they've missed the greatest opportunity of their whole lives simply because of their spiritual declension.

Please note the following: the Lord has a purpose, a design, and a plan for each and every believer, irrespective as to whom that believer is.

THE DESIGN FOR YOUR LIFE

Now, please understand very carefully that the statement we've just made is something I believe to be very important.

The Lord has a plan, a work if you will, whatever it might be, for each and every individual who has given his heart and life to Him. It doesn't matter who he is, the color of his skin, or from where he comes. It only matters as to what the Lord wants to do with him.

The first thing you should do as a believer is recognize and understand this. You were not saved to just miss hell and make heaven. You were saved to be of service to the Lord, and to be sure, He has a plan mapped out for you.

What exactly that plan is, I do not know, and most probably, you do not know either. However, you can be certain that God knows and is maneuvering you to that place, whatever that place might be, for you to be of the service for which He has called you.

Let me speak specifically of this ministry (Jimmy Swaggart Ministries), concerning the revelation of the Cross that the Lord has given us. I personally believe that every single individual who has been placed into this ministry has in some way been brought to this place and position for a purpose. I also believe that the purpose is very, very important. I am speaking of every person who watches SonLife Broadcasting Network on television, listens to SonLife Radio, or joins us on the Internet.

If the Message of the Cross is the message of this hour and the message for this generation, and I most definitely believe that it is, then any involvement in it of any nature is of extreme significance and extreme importance. You are a part of the move that the Lord is undertaking at this time, and it's all given by the Holy Spirit. We need the Lord to help us all to do His perfect will and to be exactly what He wants us to be.

The Lord called Obadiah to do something, even at the risk of his life, that he did not shrink from doing. He hasn't called us in that particular way, but He most definitely has called us. We must not fail Him!

THE TROUBLER OF ISRAEL

When Ahab met Elijah, he accused the prophet of troubling Israel. Of course, he was speaking of the terrible drought that had plagued the land. Elijah was quick to retort: *"I have not troubled Israel; but you, and your father's house, in that you have forsaken the commandments of the LORD, and you have followed Baalim"* (I Ki. 18:18).

The great prophet did not wince, did not back up, did not flinch, did not give ground, and did not temper his reply. He was not trying to curry favor, as would be overly obvious. He told it just as it was. There is no record that Ahab responded in any manner.

A cursory observation of the situation would instantly prove to anyone, at least who wanted the truth, what the problem was.

Israel was worshipping Baal. This idol god was supposed to be the god of the elements, in other words, in control of rain, storms, lightning, hail, and fire. In fact, Baal was actually the supreme deity of the heathen. In some way, all the other gods, whatever name they may have held, were a derivative of Baal. Whatever the filth, the wickedness, or the evil that was associated with this idol, the sacrifice of little children was the most hideous.

BAAL

The Hebrew noun *Ba-al* means *"master," "possessor,"* or *"husband."* Some of its names were Baal-berith, Baal-gad, Baal-hazor, Baal-meon, Baal-zebub, and Baal-zephon.

If Baal were actually real, how is it that he could not circumvent that which Jehovah had done through Elijah, such as stopping all of the rain? It would seem, would it not, that all of this was a perfect sign to Israel that they had traded Jehovah — the only true God, the maker of heaven and earth — for this monstrosity that was a figment of man's imagination and, at best, was controlled by demon spirits. However, the truth is according to what follows.

SIN IS A FORM OF INSANITY

I realize the heading is strong, but it is true. Every person in the world, in fact, every person who has ever lived who hasn't known the Lord, is a person who is ruled by insanity in some way. Sin, as stated, is a form of insanity. That means that people do not think right, do not see correctly, and do not hear correctly. As well, it means their judgment is warped and, therefore, the world is in a terrible state of war, pain, and suffering. Take a look at Islam!

While there are many religions in the world that are fueled by the powers of Satan, Islam is the worst of the lot. It is fueled by hate and carries out this hate in the form of uncontrolled murder. It hates its own people and its own devotees to Islam as much as it hates Americans or Israelis.

And yet, if it is to be noticed, in this nation of America, we suffered the loss of nearly 3,000 people on September 11, 2001. This affected tens of thousands of families and cost this nation to date probably upwards of a trillion dollars. Yet today, Muslims are still screaming hate toward us over every television station in the world that is controlled by Islam. Despite all of this just mentioned, we do not seem to understand why.

STUPIDITY

We have the ridiculous idea in our minds that if we placate these monsters, and monsters they are, somehow they will learn to love us. How stupid can we be? Once again, instead of Uncle Sam, it's becoming *"Uncle Sap."*

For instance, little children in the public schools in America are invited to learn about Islam, but no one dares mention the name of Christ because that would be against the rules. How stupid, how asinine, and how idiotic can we be?

If it is to be noticed, despite this terrible conflict in which we now find ourselves, there is very little animosity in this nation of America against the religion of Islam. We refuse to admit that it is the religion that is causing these problems. Instead, we have taken the insane direction that Islam is a wonderful religion, as the president put it sometime ago, of love and peace, which has been hijacked by a few fanatics. How long will we hide our heads in the sand? How long will we continue to play the part of being stupid? How long will we fail and refuse to recognize the true cause of all of this terrorism, which is the religion of Islam. Instead, Colin Powell, former U.S. secretary of state, exclaimed to America and the world, *"We need more Muslims in this country."* How dumb, how stupid, and how asinine such a statement is!

WHY?

Why are our smartest brains so dumb to this major threat?

When one gets to the actual reason, the problem is sin! As stated, sin is a form of insanity. That means that no matter how much education a person might have and from what school he has graduated, irrespective, if he doesn't know the Lord Jesus Christ, he will not think right, will not act right, and will not do right!

During Elijah's day, it was obvious to any believer what the problem actually was in Israel; however, Ahab didn't see it, and neither did most of Israel. It is the same today in America and Canada. We are choking Christianity to death, not realizing that it is the very source of every blessing that we have in these nations.

WARPED CHRISTIANITY!

Unfortunately, a lot that goes under the guise of Christianity falls far, far short. To be frank, all of us fall short, but in some situations, the policy of government in this country as it pertains to many Christians is totally unscriptural.

I gave an interview once to a Jewish reporter. At the first part of the conversation, he made the statement, *"You people scare me!"*

I surprised him by saying, *"I know what you're talking about, and I'm not a part of that group. They scare me as well."*

He looked very surprised and then asked me what I meant by that statement. I related my feelings to him in the following manner: If certain religious denominations and ministries had their way, they would stop everybody in this nation from preaching, unless they had the approval of the powers that be. This includes this country of America and Canada, as well. Also, it includes some ministries that are quite popular. The only thing that stops them is the Constitution of the United States.

THEY DO NOT LACK THE WILL, ONLY THE WAY

To use myself as an example: Most of that which refers to itself as Christianity in this nation would stop our ministry, and do so in totality, if they had their way. In other words, they would force us off television and radio, would close the doors of our church, etc. The only reason they don't do it is that they can't. They do not lack the will, only the way.

If they don't like the subject matter you preach, or if they cannot control you, then they want to destroy you. Let me say it again: If they had the power to do it, they would definitely do so. Just exactly as that Jewish brother said, they scare me as well!

I believe what the Bible teaches, and that is my criteria. I may disagree strongly with what somebody else preaches and teaches, and I reserve the right to cry out against it if I think it necessary to do so. However, I also reserve their right to continue to preach what they think is right. In other words, I must give them the same freedom of action as I have. I believe that's biblical and right.

For instance, I am very much opposed to Catholic doctrine, believing that it is grossly unscriptural; however, that doesn't mean that I'm opposed to Catholics, for I'm not. I'm just opposed to their religion, and, as well, I'm opposed to the doctrine of a lot of other churches!

Nevertheless, even if I had the power to do so, I would not take one step toward denying religious freedom for Catholics, or anyone else for that matter.

It must be remembered, and I know it will be hard to swallow, but it was the religious right, so to speak, who crucified Christ. While the liberals greatly opposed Him, and I speak of the Sadducees, they did not take the initiative in putting Him on the Cross. While they agreed with it and lent their support at the end, the chief opponents of Christ — those who were actually guilty of His murder — were the religious right wing, the Pharisees. It hasn't changed from then until now.

HOW LONG DO YOU HALT
BETWEEN TWO OPINIONS?

Elijah proposed a meeting on Mount Carmel, where he would stand against 450 prophets of Baal. Due to the condition of the land because of the drought, Ahab and, in fact, the entirety of Israel, in a sense, were at the mercy of Elijah. So, Ahab did not dare contest the demand of Elijah. Israel would be summoned, along with the prophets of Baal, and a contest of sorts would be enjoined.

Even though the Scripture doesn't say, more than likely, Elijah had told Ahab that God was going to send rain, but the meeting on Mount Carmel constituted some of the conditions. As stated, the condition of Israel was so dire that Ahab questioned nothing, but rather did exactly what Elijah said do. In other words, he would do about everything except repent.

It probably took several weeks for this great assembly to be brought together. No doubt, representatives from almost every household in Israel were summoned. Also, there were the 450 prophets of Baal. It is not clear if the 400 prophets of the groves came or not!

It is almost certain that the people of Israel knew that something big was in the offing. To be sure, had they known how big it actually would be, it is for certain that all who were capable of traveling would have made the journey to Mount Carmel. It would be one man against the entirety of Israel and their false prophets! What a spectacle!

The day they gathered, when everyone was finally in place, no doubt, crowding as close to the top of Mount Carmel as they could, Elijah shouted out and said, *"How long do you halt between two opinions? if the LORD be God, follow Him: but if Baal, then follow him"* (I Ki. 18:21).

The great prophet then added, *"I, even I only, remain a prophet of the LORD; but Baal's prophets are four hundred and fifty men"* (I Ki. 18:22).

As we've already stated, if anyone honestly and sincerely looks at the Word of God, the conclusion must be reached as to its validity.

The word *opinions* in the Hebrew means *"divided in mind."*

How many presently in the world are *"divided in mind"* as it regards the Lord Jesus Christ!

It is a few days from Easter as I dictate these words. How many are divided in mind as it regards the resurrection of Christ?

Whatever question one may have as it regards the Bible, concerning its miracles, its Author, or any part of the details, all are settled at the Cross. If the Cross of Christ doesn't answer every question, then the truth is not actually being sought.

The Scripture plainly says, *"For God so loved the world, that He gave His only begotten Son, that whosoever believes in Him should not perish, but have everlasting life"* (Jn. 3:16).

Calvary settles it all!

THE CROSS OF CHRIST

The Cross of Christ is the first and last savior, so to speak, between mankind and eternal hell. If the Cross is rejected, then everything else about God and His Word is rejected. Such a position settles the doom of the individual.

Concerning this very thing, Paul said, and I continue to quote from The Expositor's Study Bible: *"For it is impossible for those who were once enlightened* (refers to those who have accepted the light of the gospel, which means accepting Christ and His great sacrifice), *and have tasted of the heavenly gift* (pertains to Christ and what He did at the Cross), *and were made partakers of the Holy Spirit* (which takes place when a person comes to Christ),

"And have tasted the good Word of God (is not language that is used of an impenitent sinner, as some claim; the unsaved have no relish whatsoever for the truth of God, and see no beauty in it), *and the powers of the world to come* (refers to the work of the Holy Spirit within hearts and lives, which the unsaved cannot have or know),

"If they shall fall away (should have been translated, 'and having fallen away'), *to renew them again unto repentance* ('again' states they had once repented, but have now turned their backs on Christ); *seeing they crucify to themselves the Son of God afresh* (means they no longer believe what Christ did at the Cross, actually concluding Him to be an impostor; the only way any person can truly repent is to place his faith in Christ and the Cross; if that is denied, there is no

repentance), *and put Him to an open shame* (means to hold Christ up to public ridicule; Paul wrote this epistle because some Christian Jews were going back into Judaism, or seriously contemplating doing so)" (Heb. 6:4-6).

Paul then said:

"For if we sin willfully (the 'willful sin' is the transference of faith from Christ and Him crucified to other things) *after that we have received the knowledge of the truth* (speaks of the Bible way of salvation and victory, which is 'Jesus Christ and Him crucified' [I Cor. 2:2]), *there remains no more sacrifice for sins* (if the Cross of Christ is rejected, there is no other sacrifice or way God will accept),

"But a certain fearful looking for of judgment and fiery indignation (refers to God's anger because of men rejecting Jesus Christ and the Cross), *which shall devour the adversaries.* (It is hellfire, which will ultimately come to all who reject Christ and the Cross.)

"He who despised Moses' law died without mercy under two or three witnesses (there had to be this many witnesses to a capital crime before the death sentence could be carried out, according to the Old Testament law of Moses [Deut. 17:2-7]):

THE SPIRIT OF GRACE

"Of how much sorer punishment, suppose you, shall he be thought worthy, who has trodden under foot the Son of God (proclaims the reason for the 'sorer punishment'), *and has counted the blood of the covenant, wherewith he was sancti-*

fied, an unholy thing (refers to a person who has been saved, but is now expressing unbelief toward that which originally saved him)*, and has done despite unto the Spirit of grace?* (When the Cross is rejected, the Holy Spirit is insulted.)

"For we know Him who has said, Vengeance belongs unto Me, I will recompense, says the Lord (is meant to imply that every single thing is going to be judged by the Lord, who alone is the righteous judge). *And again, The Lord shall judge His people* (chastise His people [Deut. 32:35-36]).

"It is a fearful thing to fall into the hands of the living God. (This refers to those who have once known the Lord, but now express no faith in the Cross)*"* (Heb. 10:26-31).

Whatever the opinion might be, or whatever divides the mind, the argument is over the Cross of Christ, whether the individual understands it or not. That argument being settled, everything else, one way or the other, will fall into place.

THE GOD WHO ANSWERS BY FIRE, LET HIM BE GOD

It must be remembered that Baal claimed to be the sun god and lord of the elements and forces of nature.

It should also be remembered that in this contest, no mention was made of rain, which most would think would be the object.

Please understand that it was the Lord who was guiding Elijah as to what he must do and say. The idea is this: How much the Lord desired to show up Baal is anyone's guess.

However, His greatest thought at that time was the Cross of Calvary, which all of this represented.

The fire that came from heaven was a type of the judgment of God that would fall on Christ at the Cross, all in our stead and our place. In fact, the only thing that holds back the judgment of God on the entirety of the human race is the Cross of Christ. If that is correct, and it most definitely is, it should stand to reason that this should be the primary message of the preacher of the gospel. Regrettably, it isn't!

The modern ministry is preaching about everything except the Cross. That is tragic considering that the Cross of Christ is the only answer. It is not one answer among several, but rather it is the only answer, and that refers to anything that is wrong with the human race.

Sadly, there are very few preachers, and to be sure, very few of the laity, who really understand the Cross, at least as far as a poor human being can understand it. To be frank, the Cross is faced mostly with an attitude and spirit of unbelief.

UNBELIEF

The Cross of Christ doesn't fit with the modern gospel. It does not sit well at all with the "name it and claim it," with the motivational appeal, or with the Purpose Driven Life situation. In fact, one could name any and every other scheme that has been devised by man. Even though accepted by the church, these schemes do not sit well at all with the Holy Spirit simply because these things are the opposite of the Cross. Because the Cross lays waste all of these schemes of men, it doesn't play well in modern religious circles. In fact, it never has!

So, the modern church, at least part of it, pays lip service to the Cross and then embraces humanistic psychology or something else. Another part of the church just ignores the Cross as if it is a nonentity. Then there is the Word of Faith doctrine, which, in reality, is no faith at all. It directly repudiates the Cross, calling it *"past miseries"* and the *"worst defeat in human history."*

While it is the Lord who judges the hearts of men, which we human beings are unable to do, then I will gladly let Him do so. However, I seriously call to account the claimed salvation of that which repudiates the Cross. Again I'll state that the Lord alone can make the decision as to who is truly saved and who isn't. However, there is one thing I do know: the Word of God mitigates powerfully against those who repudiate the sacrifice of Christ (Gal. 1:8, Chpt. 5; I Cor. 1:17, 18; 2:2; Phil. 3:17-19).

NO ANSWER!

While the modern church is altogether too sophisticated to resort to the methods of the Baal worshippers of old, still, if it's not the Cross of Christ, then whatever they are doing comes under the same category. I realize that's strong, but I believe it to be true.

Please understand, when we talk about the Cross, we aren't talking about the wooden beam on which Jesus died.

We are speaking solely about what Jesus there accomplished, the price He there paid, and the great defeat of Satan and all his minions of darkness. Again I state that it's what He there did that we promote.

The Lord answers prayer or any type of petition made to Him solely on the basis of the finished work of Christ and our faith in that finished work. Otherwise, heaven is silent (Eph. 2:13-18).

I realize that there are millions today who will proverbially swear that the doctrine they have embraced, or the prattling of false apostles they have embraced, has helped them greatly, even though it is obviously unscriptural.

Have they actually been helped?

No, they have been helped not at all! Actually, they have been hurt by being kept from that which is the truth.

There are untold thousands who journey from this nation to India to sit at the feet of these so-called holy men, and they will swear that they have been greatly helped.

People do not like to be made to look foolish and, at times, will claim that whatever they're doing is right, even making themselves believe it. However, again, let us state the truth: unless the message is *"Jesus Christ and Him crucified,"* whatever it is, there will be no answer.

THE LORD DOES NOT GET GLORY OUT OF A LIE

I remember that many years ago a young man of my acquaintance claimed that the Lord had filled two of his teeth. If I remember correctly, he was claiming that they were filled with gold.

Can the Lord fill teeth?

Of course, He can!

Does He fill teeth?

There certainly might be some case in history in which He has done so; however, as it regards the fad that was making the rounds those days some years ago, no, their teeth were not being filled, at least not by the Lord. Yet, many of these individuals claimed loudly that they were.

However, let it be understood that the Lord does not get glory out of a lie! He doesn't appreciate people claiming that He has done certain things, such as the teeth-filling episode, when, in reality, He has not done such. Let us state it again: false glory is no glory at all!

The Lord is most definitely ready to give us answers; however, if we truly want answers from Him, we must go to Him in the name of Jesus (Jn. 16:23). As well, we must do so on the premise of what Christ has done for us at the Cross. The Cross alone gives us access to the very throne of God (Rev., Chpt. 5).

Incidentally, regarding the altars of Baal, the Jewish Targums state that the priests would climb into an opening that was hidden from the people and light a fire that would come up through the altar, which made it seem as if the fire had miraculously appeared. Regarding this altar of Baal that Elijah opposed, it is also stated in the Jewish Targums that something had happened to the opening through which the priests normally crawled and suffocated the man who was supposed to start the fire. Consequently, there was no fire, crooked or otherwise.

REPAIRING THE BROKEN ALTAR

The top of Mount Carmel was definitely a high place; consequently, it is obvious that there had once been an altar there as it regards the worship of the Lord. However, due to the present worship of Baal, the altar of Jehovah had long since fallen into disrepair. The truth is, with the only place of worship supposed to be at Jerusalem, there should not have been an altar on Mount Carmel to begin with. Due to the kings of Israel making it very difficult, if not impossible, for people to go to Jerusalem to worship, quite possibly this altar had been built so that some semblance of worship of the Lord could be carried forth. At any rate, Elijah would use this altar for his intended purpose.

As the great prophet repaired the altar that had long since been broken down, likewise, this is something that the modern church desperately needs to do. In other words, it needs to come back to the Cross. In every sense of the word, the Cross of Christ in the modern church has been so little preached in the last several decades that anymore, it is basically an unknown subject. That is tantamount to total disaster!

PRESENTLY, HOW CAN THE
MODERN ALTAR BE REPAIRED?

Faith is the principle that once again must be addressed. Strangely enough, there have been more books printed in the last several decades on the subject of faith than the entirety of the balance of the church put together. However, there is probably less true faith presently than ever before, at least since the Reformation.

If it's not faith in Christ and the Cross, then it's faith that God will not recognize. Tragically, most of the so-called faith exhibited presently is not at all in the Cross but in something else entirely.

The Cross of Christ, i.e., the altar, cannot be repaired by the means of legalism, and certainly not by the means of the flesh. It can only be repaired by faith once again being registered in the finished work of Christ.

How can this come about?

It can come about only as we preach the Cross, which is exactly what the Holy Spirit through Paul told us to do (I Cor. 1:18). With the Cross being preached, faith will be exercised and built up, and the power of God will once again become evident. It will register itself in changed lives, bondages of darkness being broken, and above all, souls being saved and baptized with the Holy Spirit. That and that alone is the way that the altar can be repaired. So, our prayer should be, "God give us preachers who will do as Paul when he said, '*we preach Christ crucified*'" (I Cor. 1:23).

GOD'S GOVERNMENT

The Scripture says, *"And Elijah took twelve stones, according to the number of the tribes of the sons of Jacob, unto whom the word of the LORD came, saying, Israel shall be your name"* (I Ki. 18:31).

Twelve is God's number for government, i.e., God's government, which, in effect, is His Word.

Let us say it again: His government is His Word. Every time that man goes wrong, it's when he circumvents the government of God, thereby, substituting something else to take its place. In fact, that is the sin of the church. It substitutes things of its own devising, which circumvent the Word of God and, thereby, take the church into an erroneous direction. This substitution of something else is the seedbed of apostasy.

To make it easier to understand, one might say it this way:

- From the very beginning, the world has attempted to manufacture another god other than Jehovah.
- Almost from the beginning, the church has attempted to manufacture another sacrifice.

In other words, the world wants a god of its own making, while the church wants a sacrifice of its own making. It's not satisfied with the sacrifice of Christ, so it pays lip service to His atoning work, ignores it altogether, or worse yet, repudiates that which is truly of God. Any message, any effort, and any so-called gospel other than *"Jesus Christ and Him crucified"* is that which

God can never accept. He can accept alone the sacrifice of His Son and our Saviour. Everything else is cursed (Gal. 1:8).

WITH THE STONES HE BUILT AN ALTAR

The stones, as we have stated, constituted a type of the Word of God, i.e., the government of God. They were used to build the altar, i.e., the Cross of Christ. In other words, this tells us two things:

1. The Cross of Christ is a product of the Word of God. Before the foundation of the world, God through foreknowledge knew that He would make man and that man would fall. It was deemed necessary by the Godhead that man would be redeemed by God becoming man and going to the Cross, where the price would be paid for man's redemption. This was the Word of God; this is the Word of God!

2. If the Cross of Christ is not the foundation of our message and our faith, then whatever we are believing is wrong. It must ever be understood that the Cross of Christ is not an addendum or an option. It is the foundation of all that we have from God (I Pet. 1:18-20).

THE TRENCH

Elijah dug a trench around the altar, which typified separation from the world. While the Bible in no way teaches isolation, it most definitely does teach separation. While we are in the world, we are definitely not to be of the world. As believers, there are certain things we don't do. There are certain places we don't go. There are certain things we don't talk about. Spiritually speaking, there is a trench at the edge of our faith, and we dare not go beyond the trench.

That's another problem with the modern church; it has long since obliterated the trench and adopted the ways of the world. As it regards Elijah, that trench said that everything on the inside of the trench, i.e., the altar, belonged to God. Everything outside the trench belonged to Baal. A distinction was made, even as a distinction must be made! That's the reason the Holy Spirit through Paul said, and I quote from The Expositor's Study Bible:

THE UNEQUAL YOKE

"Be not unequally yoked together with unbelievers (there are two fellowships in the world, and only two; all men belong either to one or the other; no one can belong to both and claim to be a Christian; one is with the world, and one is with the Lord)*: for what fellowship has righteousness with unrighteousness?* (None!) *and what communion has light with darkness?* (None!)

"And what concord has Christ with Belial? (This presents another name for Satan.) *or what part has he who believes with an infidel?* (Those who make a profession of salvation should resolve to separate themselves from the world. However, it is separation and not isolation.)

THE TEMPLE OF GOD

"And what agreement has the temple of God with idols? (God and idols cannot mix.) for you are the temple of the living God (speaking of all believers); as God has said (Ex. 29:45; Lev. 26:12; Ezek. 37:27), I will dwell in them, and walk in them; and I will be their God, and they shall be My people. (The believer is the sanctuary of the Holy Spirit, all made possible by the Cross.)

"Wherefore come out from among them, and be you separate, says the Lord (as stated, the Word of God emphatically teaches separation from the world, but not isolation), and touch not the unclean thing (refers to Christians avoiding all unholy contact with a vain and polluted world); and I will receive you (at the same time, means if the person disobeys these injunctions, the Lord will not receive us; the Christian can walk clean in this world only by constantly evidencing faith in the Cross of Christ, which makes it possible for the Holy Spirit to do His work within our lives).

OUR HEAVENLY FATHER

"And will be a Father unto you (but only under the conditions mentioned in the above Scriptures), and you shall be My sons and daughters, says the Lord Almighty. ('Lord Almighty' in the Hebrew is 'Jehovah Shaddai.' The Hebrew word 'Shad' means a woman's breast. The title 'Shaddai' suggests that we must never resort to the world, but rather draw all nourishment from the Lord who can provide all things, which the world can never provide.)

"*Having therefore these promises* (that we can draw all nourishment from the Lord), *dearly beloved, let us cleanse ourselves from all filthiness of the flesh and spirit* (when one sins, he sins spirit, soul, and body; there is no such thing as the body sinning, and not the spirit, etc.), *perfecting holiness in the fear of God* (to bring to a state of completion; we can do this only by 'walking after the Spirit' [Rom. 8:1-2], which refers to looking to the Cross, and looking to the Cross exclusively)" (II Cor. 6:14-18; 7:1).

THE WOOD

As is obvious, the wood symbolized the Cross.

Why did Jesus have to die on a Cross?

If He had been thrust through with a spear, would that not have sufficed?

If He had been stoned to death, would not that have sufficed?

No!

It had to be a Cross.

Why did it have to be a Cross?

The Mosaic Law stated, "*And if a man has committed a sin worthy of death, and he be to be put to death, and you hang him on a tree:*

"*His body shall not remain all night upon the tree, but you shall in any wise bury him that day; (for he who is hanged is accursed of God;) that your land be not defiled, which the* Lord *your God gives you for an inheritance"* (Deut. 21:22-23).

The idea is, only those who had committed heinous crimes were placed upon a tree. This signified that they were cursed of God.

WAS JESUS CURSED OF GOD?

The answer is no, which we will explain more readily in a moment.

The sacrifice that Jesus would offer, which would be Himself, had to atone for every sin, no matter how heinous it was. The Cross, i.e., *"the tree,"* signified the degree of such crimes.

This is the reason that the religious leaders of Israel demanded that Jesus be put on the Cross (Mat. 27:23). They knew that anyone who was justly put on the tree was accursed of God, and so they reasoned that the people would then think, were He really the Messiah, God would never allow Him to be put on a Cross.

They did not realize that the Lord had foretold the event of the Cross some 1,500 years earlier as it concerned the brazen serpent on the pole (Num. 21:8-9). It was necessary that Jesus go to the Cross in order that He might atone for all the sins of mankind, at least for all who will believe, no matter how bad those sins were (Jn. 3:16).

So, the Bible doesn't say that Jesus was accursed of God. It says that He was *"made a curse"* on the Cross, which is altogether different. Then again, He was not made a curse because of His sins, for He had none, but rather for the sin of the whole world for all time (Gal. 3:13; Jn. 1:29).

THE WORD OF GOD

To comment further upon this event of the Cross, the Scripture says, *"Christ has redeemed us from the curse of the law* (He did so on the Cross), *being made a curse for us* (He took the penalty of the law, which was death): *for it is written, Cursed is every one who hangs on a tree (Deut. 21:22-23)"* (Gal. 3:13).

As we have previously stated, if it is to be noticed, the Scripture says that Jesus was *"made a curse for us."* That is different than being cursed. He voluntarily gave Himself as a perfect sacrifice, for He was perfect in every respect. There was no sin in Him, as there had never been any sin in Him. In fact, the Scripture says of Him, *"Who is holy, harmless, undefiled, separate from sinners, and made higher than the heavens"* (Heb. 7:26). So, in order to redeem mankind, thereby, taking upon Himself the sin penalty of the whole world for all time, He had to be made a curse, which He was. The sin penalty was death.

THE JESUS DIED SPIRITUALLY DOCTRINE

It is taught by some that Jesus became a sinner on the Cross, even demon possessed, and, thereby, as such, died and went to hell as all unredeemed die and go to hell. It is claimed that He suffered the agony of the damned for some three days and nights as demons tormented Him. Then, at the end of that 72 hours, God spoke, so they say, and said, *"It is enough."* They then teach that Jesus was born again, even as a sinner is born again, and of all places, in hell. He then threw off His shackles and was raised from the dead.

There's not a shred of that in the Bible. There is no record that Jesus went to the burning side of hell. He did go down into the underworld, where He preached to the spirits in prison, which were fallen angels. As well, He delivered all who were in paradise. However, there is no record in the Word of God that Jesus went to the burning side of hell and there suffered as a sinner.

They who teach this repudiate the Cross, calling it the *"worst defeat in human history,"* thereby, referring to it as *"past miseries."* They even state that if the preacher preaches the Cross, he is preaching death, and it will destroy the people. They put no credence whatsoever in the Cross of Christ, as by now should be obvious.

NOT FOUND IN THE BIBLE

They claim that man's redemption is in the resurrection and the exaltation of Christ. So, they preach the resurrection and the throne.

None of that can be found in the Bible! It is made up out of whole cloth, so to speak.

Jesus did not die as a sinner on the Cross. If He did, how could He say, even as He did say, *"It is finished, Father, into Your hands I commend My Spirit?"* (Jn. 19:30; Lk. 23:46).

For Jesus to become a sinner would not save anyone. For Him to be tormented in hell would not save anyone. It was His sacrificial death on the Cross of Calvary that effected our salvation. This means that redemption was total and complete at the Cross.

Was the resurrection important?

Of course, it was!

However, it must be understood that if Jesus had failed to atone for even one sin, He could not have been raised from the dead. The Scripture says, *"The wages of sin is death"* (Rom. 6:23). The fact that He was resurrected proclaims the fact that all sin was atoned.

While the resurrection was of immense significance, still, it was not the cause of redemption, but rather the result of redemption (Rom. 6:5).

THE CROSS

Paul said, *"Christ sent me not to baptize, but to preach the gospel: not with wisdom of words, lest the Cross of Christ should be made of none effect"* (I Cor. 1:17).

He didn't say, *"Lest the resurrection of Christ should be made of none effect."*

He also said, *"For the preaching of the Cross is to them who perish foolishness; but unto us who are saved it is the power of God"* (I Cor. 1:18).

He didn't say, *"For the preaching of the resurrection is to them who perish foolishness ..."*

He also said, *"But we preach Christ crucified"* (I Cor. 1:23).

He didn't say that *"we preach Christ resurrected."*

To be sure, Paul did preach Christ resurrected just as we should, as well; however, as it regards salvation and all that goes with salvation, he preached the Cross.

No, Jesus did not die spiritually on the Cross. While He most definitely died, He did not die as a sinner, but rather as a sacrifice.

CUT THE BULLOCK IN PIECES

The bullock cut in pieces signified the terrible destructive power of sin.

Sin is much more than just a mere mistake and much more than a mendacity. Sin is much more than just a wrong direction or an improper effort. It is far, far more than a surface problem. The bullock was cut in pieces to signify that sin goes to the very vitals of one's being and corrupts every part and parcel of the human being. Man is born in original sin, which harks back to Adam and his fall. This means that every baby is born spiritually warped and spiritually twisted, meaning that if the child is to be saved when he reaches the age of accountability, he or she must be born again (Jn. 3:3).

This is what makes humanistic psychology, a work that originated totally with man, so absolutely ridiculous. In fact, this is what makes every single effort by religious man to assuage the problems of mankind, other than the Cross, so absolutely absurd! There are not 10, not five, and not even two solutions for sin. There is only one solution for sin, one solution for transgression, and one solution for iniquity, and that is the Cross of Christ. This is what this great illustration given to us in Chapter 18 of I Kings is telling us. We had best heed what we are being told here.

Let me say it again:

- The Cross of Christ is the *only* thing that stands between mankind and the judgment of God.
- The Cross of Christ is the *only* thing that stands between mankind and eternal hell.
- The Cross of Christ is the *only* thing that stands between the church and total apostasy.

"Hear the blessed Saviour calling the oppressed,
"O you heavy laden, come to Me and rest;
"Come, no longer tarry, I your load will bear,
"Bring Me every burden, bring Me every care."

"Are you disappointed, wandering here and there,
"Dragging chains of doubt and loaded down with care?
"Do unholy feelings struggle in your breast?
"Bring your case to Jesus, He will give you rest."

"Stumbling on the mountains dark with sin and shame,
"Stumbling toward the pit of hell's consuming flames,
"By the powers of sin diluted and oppressed,
"Hear the tender Shepherd, 'Come to Me and rest.'"

"Have you by temptations often conquered been,
"Has a sense of weakness brought distress within?
"Christ will sanctify you, if you'll claim His best,
"In the Holy Spirit He will give you rest."

ELIJAH

THE TISHBITE

CHAPTER

3

THE GREAT CONTEST

THE GREAT CONTEST

"AND HE PUT *the wood in order, and cut the bullock in pieces, and laid him on the wood, and said, Fill four barrels with water, and pour it on the burnt sacrifice, and on the wood.*

"*And he said, Do it the second time. And they did it the second time. And he said, Do it the third time. And they did it the third time.*

"*And the water ran round about the altar; and he filled the trench also with water*" (I Ki. 18:33-35).

The water was a type of the Word of God.

I hope it is obvious here that everything was saturated with water. In fact, even the trench that had been dug around the altar was filled.

This states to us that everything about the Cross was and is according to the Word of God. This tells us that the Word of God is the foundation and the criterion for all that we do. Again it states that what Jesus did at the Cross was all according to the Word of God, and according to the Word of God entirely.

Pouring the water three times over the sacrifice signifies to us that the Word of God is backed up by the entirety of the triune Godhead. It also tells us that the Word is incumbent upon each member of the Godhead, even as each member of the Godhead is incumbent upon the Word. Jesus said, *"Man shall not live by bread alone, but by every Word that proceeds out of the mouth of God"* (Mat. 4:4).

THE TIME OF THE EVENING SACRIFICE

"And it came to pass at the time of the offering of the evening sacrifice" (I Ki. 18:36).

Two sacrifices were to be offered at the temple each day, the first at 9 a.m., and the second at 3 p.m., with the latter referred to as the evening sacrifice. This was to be done seven days a week. Actually, on the Sabbath, which was Saturday, instead of one lamb being offered in the morning and one lamb in the afternoon, the number was doubled. Jesus was put on the Cross at about 9 a.m. He died at 3 p.m., the time of the evening sacrifice. So, all of this tells us that what the Lord did here was a portrayal, a picture if you will, of that which would be carried out by His Son when He died on the Cross. Of course, Elijah would have had no knowledge concerning a Cross, nor would he have known that Jesus would die on the Cross at the time of the evening sacrifice, but, of course, God most definitely did know all of this.

The idea is, the Lord was trying to bring Israel back to the altar, i.e., back to the Cross. In effect, He has always been doing this, even as He is doing such presently.

GOD OF ABRAHAM, ISAAC, AND ISRAEL

Elijah said, *"LORD God of Abraham, Isaac, and of Israel"* (I Ki. 18:36).

Why were these three individuals so special that their names would be linked with Jehovah?

One word explains it: *faith*.

At the time of these individuals, Abraham, Isaac, and Jacob (Israel and Jacob are one and the same), other than these three families at their respective times, the whole world lay in spiritual darkness. They alone knew God, and they alone believed God.

First of all, the Lord revealed Himself to Abraham. As to how this was done, the Scripture is silent. At that time, Shem, one of Noah's sons, was still alive and may very well have been serving God. Some believe that Shem was actually Melchizedek; however, there is no proof of that. At any rate, at that time, the only ones in the world who knew God were Abraham and Sarah, very probably some of Abraham's ser-vants, which definitely included Eliezer of Damascus (Gen. 14:17-20; 15:2), and a few others such as Melchizedek.

As the revelation had been given to Abraham, it was handed down to Isaac, the son of Abraham and Sarah, and then to Jacob, the son of Isaac and Rebekah.

At that time, they were the only people in the world who were monotheistic, meaning they worshipped one God, i.e., Jehovah. The balance of the world was polytheistic, meaning they worshipped many gods, in actuality, demon spirits.

So, it was faith that caused these individuals to stand out, and to be certain, faith is the same principle presently (Rom. 5:1-2).

THE FIRE OF THE LORD FELL

At the beginning of this contest, Elijah had said to Ahab, plus all of the false prophets of Baal, plus the entirety of Israel that was gathered at Mount Carmel that day, *"Let them therefore give us two bullocks; and let them choose one bullock for themselves, and cut it in pieces, and lay it on wood, and put no fire under: and I will dress the other bullock, and lay it on wood, and put no fire under:*

"And you call on the name of your gods, and I will call on the name of the LORD: and the God who answers by fire, let Him be God. And all the people answered and said, It is well spoken" (I Ki. 18:23-24).

The fire was a type of the judgment of God that was poured out on the sacrifice instead of that judgment being poured out on Israel. This typified Christ and what He would suffer at the Cross.

As we've already stated, the only thing that stands between mankind and the judgment of God is the Cross of Christ.

I Kings 18:38 says, *"Then the fire of the LORD fell, and consumed the burnt sacrifice, and the wood, and the stones, and the dust, and licked up the water that was in the trench."*

When the fire fell, it consumed everything, in effect, leaving nothing. This tells us that Calvary paid it all. No sin was left owing. The judgment was total, meaning that Christ paid it all.

Unfortunately, far too many in the modern church hypocritically seek to punish those who have failed, seemingly never realizing that Jesus has already suffered such punishment. For such to be enacted, in essence, says that what Jesus did at the Cross was insufficient. This is a gross sin! We must never forget that the *"fire of the LORD"* consumed everything — the sacrifice, the wood, the stones, and even the dust, and *"licked up the water that was in the trench."*

With all the water being licked up, this portrays the fact that the Word of God was fulfilled in totality. As stated, absolutely nothing was left owing. Such was and is the Cross of Christ!

THE LORD, HE IS THE GOD

When the fire fell, the Scripture says, *"And when all the people saw it, they fell on their faces: and they said, The LORD, He is the God; the LORD, He is the God"* (I Ki. 18:39).

Of course, these Israelites, who had been worshipping Baal for some years, were now made to realize in stark reality that Baal was not God, but rather *"the LORD, He is the God."*

The fact that the name *God* has the definite article preceding it, making it read *"the* God," tells us that, in essence, they were saying that there was no other god. Jehovah alone was God!

However, it must be understood that God, i.e., Jehovah, could only be recognized by and through the means of the Cross, i.e., the altar.

The Apostle Paul addressed this very thing, but in the New Testament sense, by stating that if the faith of believers is in anything other than Christ and the Cross, then, in essence, what they have is another Jesus, which fosters another spirit, and which plays out to another gospel (II Cor. 11:4).

This episode with Elijah and the people of Israel tells us that God could be understood only in the sense of the Cross, i.e., the altar. It is no different presently (Jn. 3:16)!

THE PROPHETS OF BAAL

"And Elijah said unto them, Take the prophets of Baal; let not one of them escape. And they took them: and Elijah brought them down to the brook Kishon, and killed them there" (I Ki. 18:40).

This is one of the reasons that the Cross is so despised. It exposes false prophets, and not only exposes them, but puts them out of business.

When the Cross of Christ is held up as it should be held up, all false doctrine goes out the window; all false apostles will stop short; all error is laid aside; and the Cross exposes it all. That's the greatest reason that the Message of the Cross is not so very much appreciated, especially considering that the majority of the modern church is apostate. The light always exposes what the darkness covers. That which the light exposes must be exterminated, which the Holy Spirit in one way or the other will definitely do, at least for those who truly want to follow the Lord.

THE RAIN OF THE SPIRIT

The people had been directed back to the Cross, of which the altar was a type, and now the rain of the Spirit could fall. Before the Holy Spirit can work, the church must come back to the Cross; there is no other way!

Seven is God's number of perfection; in other words, the rain that was coming would be in proportion to God who was sending it. Even though the Lord had promised this, we find that Elijah had to persevere. This should be a lesson to us; if we ask and we do not receive, we ought to keep asking (Lk. 11:6-13).

THE SOUND OF AN ABUNDANCE OF RAIN

When the Word of God becomes preeminent, with Calvary once again becoming the center point of all that is done, then the spiritual drought will end, and there will be an *"abundance of rain."*

As we have stated, the great drought in Israel, which had lasted now for some three and a half years, was meant to be a portrayal of the spiritual condition of the nation. The rain falling in copious amounts was a type of the Spirit of God being poured out, which brought the thirsty land back to life again, as only the Spirit of God can do. There was not merely rain that fell, but an abundance of rain.

This meant that the earth soaked up the rain, which could then once again grow grass, with the trees doing the same regarding their leaves. The streams that had long since gone dry now gurgled with water flowing in copious amounts. The drought had broken, and the rain was falling, all a type of the Holy Spirit.

However, let us once again make the statement that this copious rain was made possible by the Cross, and made possible only by the Cross. As it was then, so it is now.

The church will not know revival until it comes back to the Cross. In fact, the people, whomever they might be, will not know a touch of God in their lives until they come back to the Cross.

THE CROSS OF CHRIST

The church is not going to be helped, but rather hurt by such foolishness as the Purpose Driven Life scheme and scores of others similar.

What blasphemy is brought forth when men say that the church needs a new way, a new message, and a new presentation! No, the church needs to go back to the old paths. It needs to come back to the Cross.

The church that is truly of God does not function according to the ways of the world. That which makes the world go has no bearing whatsoever on the church, and actually, if employed, will destroy the church, which is happening presently.

The church functions solely upon the moving and operation of the Holy Spirit. The Holy Spirit works totally and completely within the confines of the finished work of Christ. So, this means that the believer must place his faith exclusively in the Cross of Christ and not allow it to be moved. With that being the case, the rain will fall in abundant amounts.

As well, this that the Lord did portrays to us the fact that if some few people will go God's way, which is the way of the Cross, beyond the shadow of a doubt, there will be an outpouring of the Holy Spirit. In fact, this experience with Elijah and the fire falling from heaven should give hope to any and every individual, irrespective of the difficulties or the problems.

HUMILITY

The Scripture says of Elijah, *"And he cast himself down upon the earth, and put his face between his knees"* (I Ki. 18:42).

Elijah had just seen one of the greatest demonstrations of power that the world had known up to that time, and it had humbled him. It was now time for the rain. The Lord had promised it. He had said some months earlier, *"Go, show yourself unto Ahab; and I will send rain upon the earth"* (I Ki. 18:1).

The answer of Elijah was actually the answer to every pulpit, every church, every home, and every problem that plagues our lives. Why is it so hard for us to do this? Why do we seek everyone's opinion and not God's knowledge? If we do seek His face, too often it is with a haughty attitude, denying all humility. God will not accept our pompous attitude. The church desperately needs revival. This verse (I Ki. 18:42) tells us how to have it. In essence, we need to cast ourselves down upon the earth and put our face between our knees. While the posture is not that important, what it represents is most definitely very important — it represents humility.

FAITH EXCLUSIVELY IN CHRIST AND THE CROSS

The Holy Spirit through Simon Peter said, *"For God resists the proud* (He sets Himself in array against the proud person)*, and gives grace to the humble* (one who places his faith exclusively in Christ and the Cross)" (I Pet. 5:5).

As the rain was dependent upon the Cross being held up as the only solution for mankind, likewise, humility is addressed in the same capacity. It is impossible for anyone to know humility unless he properly understands the Cross. The Cross of Christ is the very epitome of humility. In fact, there could be no greater example. So, when the believer begins to place his faith exclusively in Christ and the Cross, he will begin to understand a little bit about humility. Otherwise, such isn't possible!

SEVEN TIMES

"And (Elijah) *said to his servant, Go up now, look toward the sea. And he went up, and looked, and said, There is nothing. And he said, Go again seven times"* (I Ki. 18:43).

This verse portrays faith. It says, *"Go again seven times."* Regrettably, about the greatest admittance of the modern church is the admittance of the servant when he states, *"There is nothing."*

We have been compromised in our faith, being led to believe that if we snap our fingers, God is to do it immediately. If it's not done, we quit, being taught that it's not faith to continue.

That is unbiblical. No, it doesn't take the Lord long to do anything, but it takes us awhile to be brought to the place and position desired by the Holy Spirit.

Elijah was one of the greatest men of God who ever lived, but the Lord would teach even Elijah something in this episode. He would be taught a valuable lesson on the grace of God.

SEVEN TIMES SPEAKS OF A PERFECT WORK

"Seven times" speaks of God's fulfillment and completion. It speaks of a perfect work, a work that He desires to do within our lives.

In other words, if we ask and the answer is not immediately forthcoming, we must not quit. In fact, faith, that is, if it's true, will not quit. What did Jesus say?

"Which of you shall have a friend, and shall go unto him at midnight, and say unto him, Friend, lend me three loaves (a meager request);

"For a friend of mine in his journey is come to me, and I have nothing to set before him? (We as believers must give the message of eternal life to all of mankind, but the truth is, within ourselves, we have nothing to give).

"And he from within shall answer and say, Trouble me not: the door is now shut, and my children are with me in bed; I cannot rise and give to you (an obvious denial).

"I say unto you, Though he will not rise and give him, because he is his friend, yet because of his importunity he will rise and give him as many as he needs (the argument of this parable is that if a sufficiency for daily need can by importunity, i.e., persistence, be obtained from an unwilling source, how much more from a willing giver, which and who is the Lord).

EVERYONE

"And I say unto you (telling us how to approach the Lord for whatever we need), *Ask, and it shall be given you; seek, and you shall find; knock, and it shall be opened unto you* (all of this speaks of persistence and guarantees a positive answer, at least if it's in the will of God).

"For every one who asks receives; and he who seeks finds; and to him who knocks it shall be opened (he says 'everyone,' and that includes you!).

"If a son shall ask bread of any of you who is a father, will he give him a stone? or if he ask a fish, will he for a fish give him a serpent?

"Or if he shall ask an egg, will he offer him (an egg containing) *a scorpion?*

"If you then, being evil, know how to give good gifts unto your children (means that an earthly parent certainly would not give a child a stone who has asked for bread, etc.): *how much more shall your heavenly Father give the Holy Spirit to them who ask Him?"* (Lk. 11:5-13).

CHAPTER THREE **THE GREAT CONTEST** | **93**

This refers to God's goodness and the fact that everything from the Godhead comes to us through the person and agency of the Holy Spirit; and all that He does for us is based upon the Cross of Christ and our faith in that finished work.

A CLOUD THE SIZE OF A MAN'S HAND

"And it came to pass at the seventh time, that he said, Behold, there arises a little cloud out of the sea, like a man's hand" (I Ki. 18:44).

It must ever be said that what looks like only a *"little cloud"* to the unbeliever, the doubter, and the skeptic is, in fact, that which with faith can mean a coming deluge.

My grandmother taught me a most valuable lesson. I can see the twinkle in her eyes even yet. She said to me, not once but many times, *"Jimmy, God is a big God, so ask big!"*

I have never forgotten that. It has helped me touch this world for Christ.

However, we must remember that that which concludes *"big"* many times, if not most of the time, starts out small. It is only at the beginning, *"a cloud the size of a man's hand."* True faith knows that it is only the beginning, which, if God has His way, will ultimately conclude with something great. The Lord, in fact, does nothing but that which is great. Don't quit asking, don't quit seeking, and don't quit knocking.

A GREAT RAIN

"And it came to pass in the mean while, that the heaven was black with clouds and wind, and there was a great rain" (I Ki. 18:45).

One can sense the presence of God even as one reads these words, *"a great rain!"*

Spiritually speaking, our nation desperately needs this great rain. As well, spiritually speaking, untold millions of believers, myself included, need this great rain.

A PERSONAL EXPERIENCE

When the Lord began to open up to me the Message of the Cross back in 1997, it was like a dream come true. The freedom that this great truth brought to me was unexcelled. And yet, it's not something new but that which was given to the Apostle Paul, which he gave to us in his 14 epistles.

However, after a little bit, negative thoughts began to come into my mind about the necessity of the message.

The Devil said to me that while some few may need this message, virtually the entirety of the church is doing pretty well.

Looking back, it is so easy to recognize the Evil One, but at the time, dressed as an angel of light, he seemed to be plausible.

I did not reveal to anyone what I was feeling in my spirit, but the Lord was very soon to address it.

Donnie was preaching. It was Sunday night at Family Worship Center. He wasn't preaching about Moses and the deliverance of the children of Israel from Egypt, but in the course of his message, he made the statement uttered by Moses to Pharaoh, *"Let My people go."*

LET MY PEOPLE GO

When he said that word, *"Let My people go,"* the Spirit of God came all over me. I began to weep, actually sobbing, and the Lord spoke to my heart, and what He told me was not very pleasant to hear.

"My people," the Lord said, *"are in the same condition presently as the children of Israel were in Egyptian bondage."*

To be sure, that's a powerful statement. To think that the modern church is in the same shape as Israel of old, respecting Egyptian bondage, is beyond our comprehension. In other words, it's about as bad as it could ever be.

The Devil had almost made me believe that while the Cross was definitely necessary, still, the situation was not so desperate among God's people. However, that night, the Holy Spirit let me know that the church world is in the same condition, spiritually speaking, as Israel of old as it regards her terrible condition of so long, long ago. In other words, they were slaves to an evil taskmaster, and the Lord demanded, *"Let My people go."*

For a few minutes that night, I saw the entirety of the church world. I saw the bondage, and I saw untold millions who are being held captive by Satan in one way or the other, and I'm speaking of God's people. In other words, as the situation was dire in Egypt at that time, at least as it regarded the people of God, likewise, it is dire at this time. In fact, the situation is far worse than even I know.

The only answer is the Cross of Christ. There is no other! The church desperately needs a great rain of the Spirit.

"Tell me the story of Jesus,
"Write on my heart every word.
"Tell me the story most precious,
"Sweetest that ever was heard;
"Tell how the angels, in chorus,
"Sang as they welcomed His birth.
"Glory to God in the highest!
"Peace and good tidings to earth."

"Fasting alone in the desert,
"Tell of the days that He passed,
"How for our sins He was tempted,
"Yet was triumphant at last;
"Tell of the years of His labor,
"Tell of the sorrow He bore,
"He was despised and afflicted,
"Homeless, rejected, and poor."

"Tell of the Cross where they nailed Him,
"Writhing in anguish and pain,
"Tell of the grave where they laid Him,
"Tell how He lives again;
"Love in that story so tender,
"Clearer than ever I see;
"Stay, let me weep while you whisper,
"Love paid the ransom for me."

ELIJAH
THE TISHBITE

CHAPTER

4

THE THREAT OF SATAN

CHAPTER FOUR

THE THREAT OF SATAN

"THEN JEZEBEL SENT a messenger unto Elijah, saying, So let the gods do to me, and more also, if I make not your life as the life of one of them by tomorrow about this time" (I Ki. 19:2).

Ahab portrayed to Jezebel, no doubt in living color, all that Elijah had done. Jezebel then sent her threat to Elijah. The great prophet, or so she said, would be dead within 24 hours.

This is one of Satan's tactics that is very successful most of the time. As well, the threat comes in many and varied directions.

Almost immediately after a great victory in the Lord, Satan often attacks with great success. In this, we must remember that the faith of yesterday does not suffice for the need of today. The child of God must ever have a continued deposit of the touch of God, even on a daily basis. If Jezebel was so sure of her position, why did she not send soldiers to kill Elijah instead of a messenger with the threat? She did not do so because she feared for the life of the soldiers and even herself. As the fear of

Elijah was totally unfounded, so is the fear of every other child of God unfounded.

The Devil tells us that we are going to die; he tells us we're going to go bankrupt; or he tells us we're not going to make it. In other words, considering that he is lying, he can make up any story he so desires.

Empowered by oppressive spirits, for this is a spirit of oppression, it all seems to be very real. In other words, what Satan is threatening is very plausible. Circumstances point in that direction, or at least we think they do. This is something that every single child of God has had to face at one time or the other.

THE SPIRIT OF OPPRESSION

While a child of God cannot be demon possessed, the child of God can most definitely be demon oppressed. In fact, every single believer has suffered demonic oppression at one time or the other.

What is oppression?

In fact, this which we are illustrating regarding Elijah and Jezebel presents itself as a perfect example.

Oppression is carried out by demon spirits; however, it always comes from without, while demon possession comes from within. As stated, while a Christian cannot be demon possessed, a Christian can most definitely be demon oppressed.

It brings about acute fear, our emotions become affected, nerves are affected, and sometimes there are even physical problems that accompany such an attack. The person under such an attack feels like he's carrying 500 pounds on his shoulders. Despair and hopelessness, along with what seems to be helplessness, grip the individual. There seems to be no answer and no solution, and depression can be the result.

PAUL

Concerning this, Paul wrote: *"For God has not given us the spirit of fear* (refers to a disposition of the mind; the apostle is telling the young evangelist not to fear)*; but of power* (could be said, 'the spirit of power,' for such comes from the Holy Spirit)*, and of love* (again, given by the Holy Spirit)*, and of a sound mind* (a 'spirit of self-control,' all made possible by the Holy Spirit, who demands that we ever keep our faith in the Cross [Rom. 8:1-2, 11, 13])*"* (II Tim. 1:7).

The Scripture also says, *"How God anointed Jesus of Nazareth with the Holy Spirit and with power* (as a man, Christ needed the Holy Spirit, as we certainly do as well! In fact, everything He did was by the power of the Spirit)*: who went about doing good* (everything He did was good)*, and healing all who were oppressed of the Devil* (only Christ could do this, and believers can do such only as Christ empowers them by the Spirit)*; for God was with Him* (God is with us only as we are 'with Him')*"* (Acts 10:38).

THE CROSS OF CHRIST, THE ANSWER TO OPPRESSION

Sometime back, I was ministering on a Sunday morning at Family Worship Center. I was dealing with this very subject. Then, while I was preaching, it suddenly dawned on me that this problem of oppression, which almost destroyed me years ago, had not been any bother at all since the revelation of the Cross.

In other words, since the day in 1997 when the Lord began to open up to me this great truth, the very meaning of the new covenant, I have not experienced even one moment of demonic oppression. That truth was not new but was that which He had already given to the Apostle Paul. I still have very much to learn, but since that day, I have had no demonic oppression. Before that time, there were countless times that I thought I wouldn't make it. So, I know both sides of this proverbial fence. I know that the Cross of Christ is the answer.

HOW IS THE CROSS OF CHRIST THE ANSWER TO OPPRESSION?

It is there at the Cross where Satan and all of his henchmen were defeated (Col. 2:10-15; I Cor. 1:17, 18, 23; 2:2).

The Scripture says of Christ, *"And being found in fashion as a man* (denotes Christ in men's eyes)*, He humbled Himself* (He was brought low, but willingly)*, and became obedient unto death* (does not mean He became obedient to death; He was always the master of death; rather, He subjected Himself to death), *even the death of the Cross.* (This presents the character of His death as one of disgrace and degradation, which was necessary for men to be redeemed. This type of death alone would pay the terrible sin debt, and do so in totality.)

"*Wherefore God also has highly exalted Him* (to a place of supreme majesty; Jesus has always been Creator, but now He is Saviour as well), *and given Him a name which is above every name* (actually says, 'the name,' referring to a specific name and title; that name, as Verse 11 proclaims, is 'Lord'):

"*That at the name of Jesus every knee should bow* (in the sphere of the name, which refers to all it entails; all of this is a result of the Cross, the price paid there, and the redemption consequently afforded), *of things in heaven, and things in earth, and things under the earth* (all creation will render homage, whether animate or inanimate);

CONFESSION

"*And that every tongue should confess that Jesus Christ is Lord* (proclaims 'Lord' as the 'name' of Verse 9; it means 'master' of all, which again has been made possible by the Cross), *to the glory of God the Father.* (The acknowledgment of the glory of Christ is the acknowledgment of the glory of the Father)" (Phil. 2:8-11).

This doesn't mean that sometime in the illimitable future everything in heaven and earth and under the earth will bow to the Lord Jesus Christ, but rather that such has already been done.

The Scripture also says, *"And having spoiled principalities and powers* (Satan and all of his henchmen were defeated at the Cross by Christ atoning for all sin; sin was the legal right Satan had to hold man in captivity; with all sin atoned, he has no more legal right to hold anyone in bondage), *He* (Christ) *made a show of them openly* (what Jesus did at the Cross was in the face of the whole universe), *triumphing over them in it.* (The triumph is complete, and it was all done for us, meaning we can walk in power and perpetual victory due to the Cross)" (Col. 2:15).

TRIUMPH

The word *triumphing* in the Greek is *thriambeuo* and simply means *"to conquer or to give victory, to triumph over."*

This means that such victory, which was won at the Cross, is not in doubt. As well, it's a battle that will never have to be fought again.

The reason is simple: Sin, even as we have just stated, is that which gives Satan the legal right to hold man captive. With sin removed, which refers to Jesus atoning for all sin, Satan has lost his legal right to hold anyone in bondage, at least for those who will believe. He is soundly and completely defeated and has been defeated in front of the entire universe. In other words, every demon spirit is defeated, every fallen angel is defeated, and Satan himself is defeated and will be defeated forever. It was all done at the Cross!

It is intended that we have all of the victory that Christ purchased on Calvary. For the believer to have the great victory that Christ has purchased, at great price I might quickly add, the believer must place his faith exclusively in Christ and the Cross. Once this is done, the Holy Spirit, who works exclusively within the framework of the atonement, will guarantee us total victory in every capacity. In other words, the sin nature will no longer dominate us (Rom. 6:14; 8:2).

MOST BELIEVERS DO NOT REALLY UNDERSTAND THE CROSS

Most believers somewhat understand the Cross as it regards salvation but have absolutely no knowledge whatsoever as it regards sanctification, in other words, how we live for God on a daily basis. Most feel that somehow the Cross is at best something that is merely sentimental. They are fond of saying, *"Jesus died for me,"* but that's about as far as it goes. To be sure, that statement is the greatest statement that anyone could ever make, but thankfully, the Cross doesn't stop there. The truth is, every single thing we receive from God, and I mean every single thing, all and without exception is made possible by the Cross of Christ.

Most believers do not understand that our victory is predicated on the Cross. This includes our everyday walk before God, our life and living, our victory over the world, the flesh, and the Devil, the fruit of the Spirit, the gifts of the Spirit, and our growing in grace and the knowledge of the Lord.

Furthermore, most do not understand that the Holy Spirit alone can carry out these great attributes within our hearts and lives. So, not understanding that, most believers attempt to carry these things out by their own strength and volition, which guarantees failures because it is of the flesh.

WHAT THE HOLY SPIRIT ALONE CAN DO

Probably, the greatest problem the child of God faces is trying to do what the Holy Spirit alone can do. We do these things, which bring tremendous problems and trouble, simply because we do not understand the Cross as it regards our sanctification.

The believer need not suffer oppression and, in fact, will not suffer oppression if his faith is properly anchored in the Cross of Christ and remains in the Cross of Christ.

To be sure, however, this doesn't mean that Satan will stop his attacks. He will test our faith every day of the week. If we listen to him, even though we understand the Cross, we've just bought ourselves some problems.

Please remember the following: If Satan could do all of these things that he says, he would have done them a long time ago. He hasn't done them, no matter his threats, simply because he can't do them.

If he could, he would kill you. Not being able to do that, he would put you in bed for the rest of your life. Not being able to do that, he would cripple you to where you could hardly walk. However, he hasn't done any of these things, and again I state the fact, it's because he cannot do these things *"because greater is He* (the Holy Spirit) *who is in you, than he* (Satan) *who is in the world"* (I Jn. 4:4).

FEAR

"And when he saw that, he arose, and went for his life, and came to Beer-sheba, which belongs to Judah, and left his servant there" (I Ki. 19:3).

Please notice the phrase, *"And when he saw that."* It speaks of the threats that Jezebel had made against his life. Now the great prophet began to operate from a spirit of fear because of what he saw and heard instead of trusting the Lord.

However, before we criticize Elijah, we had best look at ourselves.

Would we have done any better under the circumstances? Would we have done even as well?

It's so easy to point out the weaknesses, faults, and failures of others while conveniently overlooking such in our own hearts and lives.

MOVED BY WHAT WE SEE

Yes, Elijah was grossly wrong in what he did, which, pure and simple, was a lack of trust in the Lord. However, the truth is, we fold and buckle under pressure that is not nearly as severe as that which the great prophet was facing.

At any rate, the illustration given here by the Holy Spirit is done so for our benefit in order that we may learn not to do what Elijah did.

Regrettably, it seems that despite the illustration, we learn very slowly, if at all.

Back to the phrase, *"And when he saw that,"* it addresses itself to our biggest problem. It is so easy to be moved by what we see and what we hear, in other words, the obvious. We should not be moved by these things, whether they are good or bad. Our action, that which we do, our life and living, and as Paul referred to it, *"our walk,"* must be decided on the basis of the Word of God and nothing else. What does the Word say? What does the Lord tell us? That and that alone must be our criterion. If we do not have a word from the Lord as to what direction we are to go, we should stay where we are until that word makes itself obvious.

If we function according to what other people say or according to circumstances, in other words, according to what we can see, we are going to take a wrong path, and a wrong path taken will not come out right.

PRESUMPTION

At the same time, we must not be ruled by presumption. This pertains to an attitude or a belief dictated by probability. It is a legal inference as to the existence or truth of a fact not certainly known that is drawn from the known or proved existence of some other fact. In other words, it's not wise at all to follow such a course.

The sin of presumption is what Satan tried to get our Lord to commit. The Scripture says, *"Then the Devil took him up* (a powerful force) *into the Holy City* (Jerusalem)*, and set him on a pinnacle of the temple* (it's highest point, which Josephus stated, was about 700 feet from the highest point of its wall to the lowest point of the ravine below),

"And said unto Him, If you be the Son of God (since You are the Son of God)*, cast Yourself down* (literally spoken)*: for it is written, He shall give His angels charge concerning You: and in their hands they shall bear You up, lest at any time You dash Your foot against a stone* (this was derived from Psalms 91:11-12)*"* (Mat. 4:5-6).

OUR DESIRES MUST BE GOD'S DESIRES

It is true that the Scripture does say that the angels would protect our Lord while He was in incarnate form, i.e., human form. However, if Jesus had done what Satan tempted Him to do, it would have been sin.

The idea was that Jesus could do this thing, in other words, engage in this stunt, and people would then accept Him. However, the angels would protect Him only as long as He was carrying out the will of God, and to be sure, the Holy Spirit in no way had told our Lord to carry out this stunt.

We have many people who read a verse in the Word of God and then go out and try to use that verse to claim something that the Lord doesn't want for them.

Jesus said, *"What things soever you desire, when you pray, believe that you receive them, and you shall have them"* (Mk. 11:24).

The actual meaning of this text is that our desires must be God's desires. Whenever we ascertain that something is His will for our lives, then the Scripture applies. To be sure, it is not a blank check for a believer to chart his own course. The very heart of the gospel is, *"Not my will, but Your will, be done"* (Lk. 22:42).

While the Word of God is to be the criterion for all things within our hearts and lives, and not things that we see or observe, still, the Word must be rightly understood and rightly applied.

FEAR AND THE CROSS OF CHRIST

We teach that the Cross of Christ is the answer and the solution to every problem that man has. If the reader follows my teaching to any degree at all, it will soon become obvious that we place the Cross of Christ as the solution for all things. It doesn't matter if it's humility, sin, consecration, victory, or in this case, fear, the answer is the Cross, and the answer alone is the Cross. Here is a valuable lesson that we should learn.

Elijah had just been given the greatest demonstration of the power of the Cross that anyone could ever have. At the behest of the Lord, he had repaired the altar that had been broken down, which was a type of the Cross. The prophet had witnessed the fire fall from heaven, which signified God's acceptance of His Son and our Saviour, the Lord Jesus Christ, as it regarded the sacrifice that He would offer. So, he knew, at least as far as one could know under the old covenant, that the Cross was the answer.

Of course, the word *Cross* would not have been in his vocabulary. In fact, he would not have even known what such meant. However, he did most definitely understand the altar and what it represented in that it pointed to One who was to come, who would redeem fallen humanity. I am positive this was very clear to the great prophet, but now, he succumbed to fear.

He had witnessed what the altar, i.e., the Cross, did to the prophets of Baal. He witnessed what it did to the people of Israel. He witnessed as to the great rain that broke the drought, which followed the demonstration of the altar. Yet, he didn't seem to understand that which was sufficient in such a grand way for the wayward nation of Israel was also sufficient for him presently.

THE CROSS OF CHRIST AND THE INDIVIDUAL

In defense of Elijah, as is obvious, he lived under the old covenant. As a result, while the Holy Spirit most definitely was in him in order that these great miracles would be carried out, still, this had little or nothing to do with Elijah's everyday living for God. In other words, he didn't have the privileges that we have under the new covenant. Due to the Cross now being a fact, the Holy Spirit abides within our hearts and lives permanently. He not only helps us to do certain things regarding the miraculous, but above all, He helps us to live as we ought to live by using His power on our behalf (Jn. 14:16-17; 16:7-15; Acts 1:8).

While Elijah did have the example of the Cross to speak before him, still, as stated, in truth, he didn't have nearly the help that we presently have. Our help is all due to the fact that now the Cross is an accomplished work, which gives the Holy Spirit great latitude within our lives. The idea is, while there was no excuse for Elijah to do what he did, still, there is even less excuse for us now.

DAILY LIVING FOR VICTORY

For the few of you who do understand the Cross of Christ as it regards our daily living, let me warn you that for victory to be maintained, it is still necessary for you to heed the words of Christ. He said:

"If any man will come after Me (the criterion for discipleship), *let him deny himself* (not asceticism as many think, but rather that one denies one's own willpower, self-will, strength, and ability, depending totally on Christ), *and take up his cross* (the benefits of the Cross, looking exclusively to what Jesus did there to meet our every need) *daily* (this is so important, our looking to the Cross, that we must renew our faith in what Christ has done for us, even on a daily basis, for Satan will ever try to move us away from the Cross as the object of our faith, which always spells disaster), *and follow Me* (Christ can be followed only by the believer looking to

the Cross, understanding what it accomplished, and by that means alone [Rom. 6:3-5, 11, 14; 8:1-2, 11; I Cor. 1:17-18, 21, 23; 2:2; Gal. 6:14; Eph. 2:13-18; Col. 2:14-15]).

"For whosoever will save his life shall lose it (try to live one's life outside of Christ and the Cross): *but whosever will lose his life for My sake, the same shall save it* (Jn. 10:10)" (Lk. 9:23-24).

When we place our faith entirely in Christ and what He did for us at the Cross, looking exclusively to Him, we have just found more abundant life (Jn. 10:10; Lk. 9:23-24).

The idea is, even as Jesus gave us this admonition, all of this is so important that, in a sense, we must renew our faith in Christ and the Cross on a daily basis.

THE CROSS AND OUR FAITH

Our Lord continued to say: *"And whosoever does not bear his Cross* (this doesn't speak of suffering as most think, but rather ever making the Cross of Christ the object of our faith; we are saved and we are victorious not by suffering, although that sometimes will happen, or any other similar things, but rather by our faith, but always with the Cross of Christ as the object of that faith), *and come after Me* (one can follow Christ only by faith in what He has done for us at the Cross; He recognizes nothing else), *cannot be My disciple* (the statement is emphatic! If it's not faith in the Cross of Christ, then it's faith that God will not recognize, which means that such people are refused)" (Lk. 14:27).

I would hope that the reader is doing more than giving these statements by Christ a cursory glance. Bluntly and plainly, our Lord has said that if we do not take up the Cross daily, we simply cannot be His disciple.

This is the reason the great Apostle Paul said, *"But though we, or an angel from heaven, preach any other gospel unto you than that which we have preached unto you* (Jesus Christ and Him crucified)*, let him be accursed* (eternally condemned; the Holy Spirit speaks this through Paul, making this very serious)" (Gal. 1:8).

- There is no salvation outside of the Cross of Christ.
- There is no victory in life and living outside of the Cross of Christ.
- There is no overcoming power outside of the Cross of Christ.
- There is no development of the fruit of the Spirit outside of the Cross of Christ.
- There is no leading and guidance of the Holy Spirit outside of the Cross of Christ.
- In fact, as it pertains to God, there is nothing outside of the Cross of Christ.

A PRAYER THAT GOD WOULD NOT ANSWER

The great prophet now said, *"It is enough; now, O LORD, take away my life"* (I Ki. 19:4).

We are looking here at total despair! Let the reader understand that Elijah's problem was not merely the threat of Jezebel, as real as that was, or any other thing that one might think. This was a direct attack by the powers of darkness against the great prophet, as stated, a spirit of oppression.

As should be obvious, while living for the Lord is the greatest life there is and the most fulfilled life there is, still, we are not immune from attacks by the powers of darkness.

Even the great Paul experienced something similar.

Due to false apostles and trouble at the church in Corinth, it looked for a little while as if the church there might be lost.

He had sent his first epistle (I Corinthians) to the church and had been rather strong in some of his statements. He was greatly concerned that quite possibly they would not accept the things that he said. Not able to go to Corinth at that time himself, he sent Titus. It was planned that he would meet Titus at Troas at a certain time, with Titus giving him news of the church; however, when Paul arrived at Troas, Titus evidently had been delayed and was not there (II Cor. 2:12-13).

DEMONIC OPPRESSION

Paul had evidently become so distraught over the situation that even though he had an opportunity to minister at Troas, he simply could not do so.

It's very easy for us presently to look at the situation and to chide Paul, claiming that he should have trusted the Lord and not worried about the situation. All of that is true, but again, it is not wise for us to make snap judgments. In the first place, if Corinth had been lost, due to several factors, it could have had a domino effect on many other churches as well. We must understand that Paul was being contested by false apostles on a continual basis. It was a problem that he faced constantly. Now it looked as if Corinth was going to go astray, which would hinder the entirety of the move of God as it regarded the establishing of the church, for which Paul was responsible. At any rate, Paul was so concerned, and that's a mild word, that for a period of time, he was unable to function as he should. Thankfully, when he finally did see Titus, the news was not negative but very positive. The church at Corinth had accepted his admonition as it regarded the epistle of I Corinthians.

LIVING FOR THE LORD

Living for the Lord, at least properly so, is not a simple task. While it is the greatest life, and by far the most fulfilled life there is, still, unless it is done God's way, and His way exclusively, we are going to run into real problems. Consequently, there are at least two major difficulties, and we are speaking of the true believer who really loves the Lord and desires to do His will.

The first problem is the learning process.

When the believing sinner comes to Christ and is instantly born again, he enters into a dimension of life and living that he never knew existed. As stated, it is truly *"joy unspeakable and full of glory"* (I Pet. 1:8).

Very shortly after his coming to Christ, in some way, he will fail the Lord. In fact, there have been no exceptions to this.

Upon that occasion, he is greatly shocked and hurt that he has done so. In other words, he has sinned.

As a new convert, and regrettably, most older converts, as well, he has no knowledge whatsoever of the sin nature. In fact, before his conversion, the sin nature ruled him 24 hours a day, seven days a week.

However, when he came to Christ, in a moment's time, actually at the occasion of the new birth, the sin nature was made ineffective (Rom. 6:6). In other words, he was no longer controlled by the sin nature as he once was but was now controlled by the divine nature.

THE DIVINE NATURE

The Scripture says, *"According as His divine power has given unto us all things* (the Lord with large-handed generosity has given us all things) *that pertain unto life and godliness* (pertains to the fact that the Lord Jesus has given us everything we need regarding life and living), *through the knowledge of Him who has called us to glory and virtue* (the 'knowledge' addressed here speaks of what Christ did at the Cross, which alone can provide 'glory and virtue')*:*

"Whereby are given unto us exceeding great and precious promises (pertains to the Word of God, which alone

holds the answer to every life problem): *that by these* (promises) *you might be partakers of the divine nature* (the divine nature implanted in the inner being of the believing sinner becomes the source of our new life and actions; it comes to everyone at the moment of being 'born again'), *having escaped the corruption that is in the world through lust.* (This presents the salvation experience of the sinner and the sanctification experience of the saint)" (II Pet. 1:3-4).

Upon failure, the believer then sets out to find a way so that the failure will not be repeated. This is where the trouble begins.

Not understanding the Cross, most make attempts to guarantee a life of victory by any number of ways, all of them wrong. When this happens, which is actually a state of spiritual adultery, the Holy Spirit is now greatly hindered in helping that individual. While He will most definitely do all that He can, He cannot involve Himself in spiritual adultery.

WHAT IS SPIRITUAL ADULTERY?

Paul dealt with this subject in Romans 7:1-4.

To be brief, he speaks of a woman who is married to a man. She then marries another man while still married to the first man. Paul said, *"She shall be called an adulteress"* (Rom. 7:3).

Now, why did he use such an illustration?

He was telling us that we as believers are married to Christ. As such, spiritually speaking, Christ is our husband (Rom.

7:1-4; II Cor. 11:1-4). Also, as such, He is to meet our every need and, in fact, is the only One who can meet our every need. However, when we cast about to try to find victory in some way other than total faith in Him and what He did for us at the Cross, we are actually being unfaithful to our Lord, i.e., *"our husband,"* which means that we are committing spiritual adultery. Now we are deprived of the help of the Holy Spirit.

HOW THE HOLY SPIRIT WORKS

To have the help of the Holy Spirit, which all of us must have, that is, if we are to be what we ought to be in Christ, our faith must be anchored firmly in the Cross of Christ. The Holy Spirit demands that (Rom. 6:1-14; 8:1-11; I Cor. 1:17-18, 23; 2:2; Gal., Chpt. 5; 6:14; Col. 2:10-15).

As long as we keep our faith anchored solely in the Cross of Christ and not allow it to be moved elsewhere, the Holy Spirit will use His almighty power on our behalf, and the sin nature will remain ineffective. However, the moment that we put our faith in something other than the Cross of Christ, this stops the Holy Spirit from helping us, thereby, leaving us on our own, which guarantees failure on our part. In fact, regrettably, almost the entirety of the church world is struggling in this very area simply because they do not understand the sin nature. Neither do they understand how the Holy Spirit works, which means they do not understand the Cross relative to sanctification. So, their life and living constitute a cycle of failure and repentance, failure and repentance, etc.

THAT IS NOT GOD'S WAY

Until that new convert understands the Cross of Christ as it refers to his daily life and living, he is going to struggle greatly in this area, with the sin nature once again ruling him in some way.

That's why Paul also said: *"Let not sin* (the sin nature) *therefore reign* (rule) *in your mortal body* (showing that the sin nature can once again rule in the heart and life of the believer, if the believer doesn't constantly look to Christ and the Cross; the 'mortal body' is neutral, which means it can be used for righteousness or unrighteousness), *that you should obey it in the lusts thereof* (ungodly lusts are carried out through the mortal body, if faith is not maintained in the Cross [I Cor. 1:17-18])" (Rom. 6:12).

If it were not possible for the sin nature to once again rule and reign within our mortal bodies, i.e., our lives, then Paul would not have given us this warning.

Let us say it again: if we function according to the Word of God, thereby, placing our faith and confidence in Christ and what He has done for us at the Cross, and maintaining our faith in that finished work, we are then guaranteed the help of the Holy Spirit, which will guarantee us having and living the more abundant life (Jn. 10:10).

FRUSTRATING THE GRACE OF GOD

Due to the fact that the Cross of Christ has been so little preached in the last few decades, most modern believers have no understanding at all of the things we have just discussed. That is tragic because this means they are not living a victorious life.

Let me make this statement: It is impossible for any believer, and I don't care who that believer is — the greatest preacher in the world, the pastor with the largest church, or the evangelist with the biggest crowds — to live a victorious life outside of faith in Christ and the Cross. It simply cannot be done.

The great Paul also said: *"I do not frustrate the grace of God* (if we make anything other than the Cross of Christ the object of our faith, we frustrate the grace of God, which means we stop its action, and the Holy Spirit will no longer help us): *for if righteousness come by the law* (any type of law), *then Christ is dead in vain.* (If we can successfully live for the Lord by any means other than faith in Christ and what He did for us at the Cross, then the death of Christ was a waste)" (Gal. 2:21).

The believer must understand that any method we choose, any direction we take as it regards living for God, or anything other than faith in Christ and the Cross is looked at by the Lord as law, whether we understand such or not.

WHAT IS LAW?

If it is to be noticed, the Apostle Paul talked about law constantly. Why did he do this, especially considering that most of his converts were Gentiles, meaning that they had no understanding whatsoever of the law of Moses?

As well, considering that Jesus fulfilled the law, and did so in every respect, why did Paul make such an issue of this principle? After all, we are now living under the new covenant, which means that the law is no more incumbent upon believers.

First of all, Paul didn't write these epistles according to what he thought about things. He was moved upon by the Holy Spirit, who even chose and selected each word used by the apostle. So, what he wrote was the Word of God. To be sure, the Holy Spirit had a reason for dealing with law as He did.

The whole of the human race is either under law or grace. In fact, every unsaved person in the world who has ever lived is under law. That means that at the great white throne judgment, they will answer to God according to the moral law. We're speaking of the law of Moses, and more specifically, the Ten Commandments (Ex., Chpt. 20).

LAW AND GRACE

When the believing sinner comes to Christ, he comes from the position of law to the position of grace, all afforded by Christ. We are to operate totally under the principle of grace, once again, all afforded by Christ and what He did for us at the Cross.

However, the only way, and I mean the only way, the believer can function on and in the principle of grace is by placing his faith exclusively in Christ and the Cross. It cannot be done any other way. This is demanded of every believer (incidentally, grace is simply the goodness of God extended to undeserving believers).

CRUCIFIED WITH CHRIST

Paul said, *"I am crucified with Christ* (as the foundation of all victory; Paul, here, takes us back to Romans 6:3-5)*: nevertheless I live* (have new life)*; yet not I* (not by my own strength and ability)*, but Christ lives in me* (by virtue of me dying with Him on the Cross and being raised with Him in newness of life)*: and the life which I now live in the flesh* (my daily walk before God) *I live by the faith of the Son of God* (the Cross is ever the object of my faith)*, who loved me, and gave Himself for me* (which is the only way that I could be saved)*"* (Gal. 2:20).

If it is to be noticed, when the great apostle told us how to live for God, which was really the Holy Spirit speaking through Him, He first of all took us straight to the Cross: *"I am crucified with Christ."*

Now, let me say it again: if the believer doesn't place his faith exclusively in Christ and the Cross, and that means that we are trusting in nothing else to help us live this life, then such a believer is automatically going to be in law whether he understands such or not.

LAWS DEVISED BY MEN

When we speak of law, if it's traced properly, it will always go back to the law of Moses, and again we speak of the Ten Commandments. Still, it also includes all of the laws that we devise out of our own minds.

Let me give an example: the other day I saw a preacher over television telling people that for whatever problem they had, if they would take the Lord's Supper, even if they had to take it every day, this would guarantee them victory.

The Lord's Supper is most definitely a scriptural ordinance, which means that it's something that every believer should do. Still, taking the Lord's Supper is not going to guarantee any victory whatsoever. Do you find such in the Bible? No, you don't!

So, I do not doubt his good motives, but what was happening was that this dear brother was actually taking people to law. In other words, he was making a law out of this divine ordinance, which Christ never intended. Because what is being suggested is good, and the Lord's Supper is definitely good, it fools us into believing that it is right. It isn't.

FASTING

A book was written sometime back on the subject of fasting. The writer said that if a person would fast 21 days (or some such number), that would give him victory over evil, etc. Now, while fasting is most definitely scriptural and will certainly bless the individual, it will not give anyone victory over sin. The preacher in question, and again, I do not doubt his motives, was making a law out of fasting, which God can never honor. While fasting is a great discipline and should be engaged as the Lord leads us, there will not be any victory over sin gained in this manner.

The answer to sin, addiction, or any problem of this nature is not in anything except the Cross of Christ. It was there that victory was won by Christ, and Satan was defeated (Heb. 2:14-15).

Now, don't let the reader think that we are demeaning fasting. We aren't, not at all! We are attempting, however, to place the emphasis where it should be placed, which is on the Cross of Christ.

FIGHT THE GOOD FIGHT OF FAITH

The second problem the believer faces, and I'm speaking of the believer who knows and understands the Cross of Christ, is Satan attempting to move his faith from the Cross to other things. Don't think that just because you are aware of the Cross and its implications that Satan will fold his tent and slink away. He won't! In fact, he's going to come against you with everything he has, in effect, trying your mettle, so to speak, and the Lord will allow him that latitude.

The truth is, none of us has faith quite as strong as we think we do. The temptations allowed by the Evil One will prove our faith, showing us that it's not as strong as it ought to be. This will enable us to take the necessary steps that we must take in order to properly grow in grace and the knowledge of the Lord.

THE ONLY FIGHT

Paul told Timothy, *"Fight the good fight of faith* (in essence, the only fight we're called upon to engage; every attack by Satan against the believer, irrespective of its form, is to destroy or seriously weaken our faith; he wants to push our faith from the Cross to other things), *lay hold on eternal life* (we do such by understanding that all life comes from Christ, and the means is the Cross), *whereunto you are also called* (called to follow Christ), *and have professed a good profession before many witnesses.* (This does not refer to a particular occasion, but to the entirety of one's life for Christ)" (I Tim. 6:12).

The trouble with most of Christendom is that it is fighting a fight that it doesn't need to fight and, in fact, should not fight.

FIGHTING AGAINST SIN

Let me give an example: Sin was settled at the Cross. There the Lord Jesus Christ atoned for any, all, and every sin, and for all time, at least for all who will believe (Jn. 3:16). So, our fight is not really with sin. Our fight is, as stated, *"the good fight of faith."*

When the believer fights against sin in any capacity, such shows that he doesn't understand the Cross, meaning that he doesn't understand what Jesus there did. So, if we start fighting against sin, we have stated, whether we realize it or not, that what Jesus did at the Cross was insufficient, and we have to add our effort to what He has already done. As should be obvious, this doesn't sit well with the Holy Spirit! The work of Christ is a finished work, meaning that nothing is left undone.

Satan is very pleased to maneuver us into a place and position to where we are fighting sin. It makes us feel good, despite the fact that we always lose. In fact, with some Christians, their entire life is a life of struggle, and they think that somehow, such constitutes holiness. It doesn't!

There is a struggle, in fact, but it's the struggle of faith. Let us never forget that (Rom. 5:1-2).

THE ANGEL OF THE LORD

"And as he lay and slept under a juniper tree, behold, then an angel touched him, and said unto him, Arise and eat" (I Ki. 19:5).

Despite the condition of the great prophet, despite his faithlessness, despite him going in the wrong direction, and despite his failure of trust in the Lord, still, the *"angel of the Lord"* was with him every foot of the journey, despite its wrong direction. This should be a consolation to us.

Instead of the Lord answering his prayer as it regarded taking his life, He instructed the angel to give him some miracle food and miracle water.

We are given very little information regarding this incident, and none at all as to Elijah's reaction. To be frank, quite possibly, he didn't even know it was an angel at the beginning, and then, maybe he did. At any rate, he partook of the bread and the water.

Evidently, he didn't eat enough, so the angel touched him the second time, saying to him, *"Arise and eat; because the journey is too great for you"* (I Ki. 19:7).

Thank the Lord that He doesn't leave us even though we at times go wrong. As the Lord was watching over the prophet, likewise, He watches over each and every one of us.

The truth is, Elijah probably would have died but for the visitation of the angel. However, the Lord most definitely wasn't through with him and still isn't through with him even yet.

THE MINISTRY OF ANGELS

The question begs to be asked, *"Are there visitations of angels presently even as it was during the time of Elijah?"*

Yes!

Paul wrote, *"Be not forgetful to entertain strangers* (hospitality)*: for thereby some have entertained angels unawares* (definitely would have a tendency to provide a positive incentive)*"* (Heb. 13:2).

While visitations from angels do not occur very often, the occasion mentioned, regarding Elijah's life and ministry, is the only incident of which we are aware; however, it does happen.

Paul also wrote, *"Are they not all ministering spirits* (the function of angels)*, sent forth to minister for them who shall be heirs of salvation?* (This proclaims that angels attend only those who have made Christ their Saviour)*"* (Heb. 1:14).

This tells us that angels, although unseen, are sent to minister (to serve) to all believers. Although they do not often make themselves known or visible, the Scriptures tell us, nevertheless, they are present.

A HUNDRED AND EIGHTY MILES
FROM THE JUNIPER TREE

Horeb, where Elijah was now, was about 180 miles from where he had sat under a juniper tree. Evidently, the food prepared for him by the angel was supernatural and provided a supernatural strength. The Scripture says, *"And he arose, and did eat and drink, and went in the strength of that meat forty days and forty nights unto Horeb the mount of God"* (I Ki. 19:8).

Even though it cannot be proven, there is a possibility that the cave where Elijah arrived was the cleft of the rock in which Moses had stood while the Lord passed by (Ex. 33:22). He had come all this distance, and now the Lord asked him why he was there.

WHAT ARE YOU DOING HERE, ELIJAH?

Even though the Lord through the angel greatly helped the prophet, as is here obvious, still, the help given by the Lord didn't mean that Elijah was in the will of God. In fact, the very question posed by the Lord to the prophet, *"Why are you here, Elijah?"* (I Ki. 19:9) proclaims the fact that none of this was the Lord's doing.

What would the answer be if the Lord asked every believer presently, *"What are you doing here?"*

Concerning this very thing as it pertains to the new covenant, Paul said, *"Examine yourselves, whether you be in the faith* (the words, 'the faith,' refer to 'Christ and Him crucified,' with the Cross ever being the object of our faith); *prove your own selves.* (Make certain your faith is actually in the Cross and not in other things.) *Know you not your own selves, how that Jesus Christ is in you* (which He can only be by our faith expressed in His sacrifice), *except you be reprobates?* (Rejected)" (II Cor. 13:5).

Any place in which the believer might find himself other than *"in the faith"* deserves the question, *"What are you doing here?"*

So many of the journeys that we take are so useless, so out of order, and so unnecessary! More than likely, that could be said of all of us.

THE STATE OF ELIJAH

In reply to the question asked by our Lord, the prophet at once began to speak well of himself and ill of the nation. Concerning this, George Williams said, *"He should have set himself aside and interceded for, and not against Israel, as Romans, Chapter 11, teaches. He was angry because the people would not listen to him and turn unto Jehovah."*

Williams went on to say, *"The angry prophet, crouching with embittered heart in the cavern, pictured the nation. The 'flesh' in him was just as hateful as the 'flesh' in them. He was invited to come forth and meet God. He refused; he must therefore be compelled to come forth."*

What was the Lord showing the prophet as it regarded the demonstrations?

THE WIND, THE EARTHQUAKE, AND THE FIRE

The answer of the Lord to the prophet was a tempest that did rend the mountains, followed by an earthquake, and then a fire. However, the Scripture emphatically states that Jehovah was not in these. This means that the prophet could neither be burnt out nor forced out. Then there comes the stillness, which occasioned *"a still small voice."*

Concerning this, the Scripture says: *"And it was so, when Elijah heard it, that he wrapped his face in his mantle, and went out, and stood in the entering in of the cave."* Then the voice spoke again and said, *"What are you doing here, Elijah?"* (I Ki. 19:13).

Williams goes on to say, *"Had his heart not been occupied with self, he would have learned that tempests, earthquakes and fires cannot accomplish what the gentle voice of love can. He should have recognized that there was no difference between his heart and that of the nation; and that as force failed to make him leave his cave, so it failed, and must fail to compel men to leave their sins."*

SLOW TO LEARN, BUT AREN'T ALL OF US?

However, he was slow to learn. When asked again, *"What are you doing here, Elijah?"* he repeated his angry and foolish words and interceded not for Israel, but rather against Israel.

The prophet had told the Lord, *"And I, even I only, am left"* (I Ki. 19:14), as it regarded those in Israel who were living for the Lord. The Lord gently and kindly told him, *"Yet I have left Me seven thousand in Israel, all the knees which have not bowed unto Baal, and every mouth which has not kissed him"* (I Ki. 19:18).

Our blessed Saviour is our example. While He hated the sin, He loved the sinners.

In this ministry (Jimmy Swaggart Ministries), we are not opposed to alcoholics; we are opposed to alcoholism. We are not opposed to homosexuals; we are opposed to homosexuality. We are not opposed to gamblers; we are opposed to gambling, etc.

As wonderfully as the great prophet was used by the Lord as it regarded the repairing of the altar and the fire falling from heaven, he seemed to have little learned the lesson taught by the Cross, of which the altar was a type. That lesson is simple!

"For God so loved the world, that He gave His only begotten Son, that whosoever believes in Him should not perish, but have everlasting life" (Jn. 3:16).

THE MANTLE OF ELIJAH

Nearby was a school of the prophets, but upon none of these did Elijah cast his mantle. Guided by the Holy Spirit, he cast it upon a plowboy. How different are God's thoughts from man's! He chose Amos, who was a gatherer of sycamore fruit, and Paul, who was not one of the Twelve, and Moody, who was uneducated. Through men like these, He rebukes and refreshes the *"official ministry."*

THE CALLING OF ELISHA

Elijah left Horeb and found one of these 7,000 mentioned by the Lord, i.e., Elisha.

As is obvious, the Lord chose Elisha to take the place of Elijah, at least when Elijah would be translated. Of course, it is very doubtful that the great prophet then knew or understood that he, in fact, would not die but would be translated. Actually, it would be some 10 years before this great occasion.

From the words, *found Elisha*, it is implied that Elijah didn't really even know this young man and had to search him out. That should not have been difficult as the Lord had told him, *"And Elisha the son of Shaphat of Abel-meholah shall you anoint to be prophet in your room"* (I Ki. 19:16).

So, the prophet found Elisha and *"cast his mantle upon him,"* even though he was then plowing with oxen.

What we're seeing here is God's way as it regards His call upon the hearts and lives of those whom He would choose. At the present time, too many individuals are in the ministry who have called themselves. As a result, there is no anointing upon their ministry, as should be obvious.

The Lord anoints only those whom He has called, and that anointing is very, very special, as should be obvious.

THE ANOINTING

As well, it should be understood that no individual can give his anointing, at least should he have such, to someone else. That is strictly and totally the prerogative of the Lord. It is unfortunate that at the present time, we have preachers who claim that they can give their anointing to others, and irrespective of the manner in which it is suggested, all the time, it amounts to money. In other words, *"If you give me money, I will give you my anointing."*

I think it can be said scripturally, without any fear of exaggeration or contradiction, that any preacher who would attempt such, whatever he might have had in the past, if anything, he no longer has it presently. While prophets and preachers were and are used of God to recognize those whom God has already called, all that they can do is to recognize the calling. It is the Lord and only the Lord who does the anointing.

Paul wrote, *"But the manifestation of the Spirit is given to every man to profit withal"* (I Cor. 12:7). This means, as stated, it is the Spirit of God who does the giving, and not man.

I heard a preacher over television say, *"If you will come join my group,"* or words to that effect, *"you will come under my anointing."* As well, there was a certain sum of money they had to give!

No, they won't!

I'll say it again: if that preacher did once have the anointing, it is guaranteed that it is something that he no longer possesses.

PREACHERS AND PEOPLE

The truth is, every believer is going to follow some preacher. In fact, the Scripture says, *"And He gave* (our Lord does the calling) *some, apostles* (has reference to the fact that not all who are called to be ministers will be called to be apostles; this applies to the other designations as well; 'apostles' serve as the de facto leaders of the church, and do so through the particular message given to them by the Lord for the church); *and some, prophets* (who stand in the office of the prophet, thereby, foretelling and forthtelling); *and some, evangelists* (to gather the harvest); *and some, pastors* (shepherds) *and teachers* (those with a special ministry to teach the Word to the body of Christ; 'apostles' can and do function in all of the callings);

THE PERFECTING OF THE SAINTS

"For the perfecting of the saints (to 'equip for service'), *for the work of the ministry* (to proclaim the message of redemption to the entirety of the world), *for the edifying of the body of Christ* (for the spiritual building up of the church):

"Till we all come in the unity of the faith (to bring all believers to a proper knowledge of Christ and the Cross), *and of the knowledge of the Son of God* (which again refers to what He did for us at the Cross), *unto a perfect man* (the believer who functions in maturity), *unto the measure of the stature of the fullness of Christ* (the 'measure' is the 'fullness of Christ,' which can only be attained by a proper faith in the Cross):

"That we henceforth be no more children (presents the opposite of maturity, and speaks of those whose faith is in that other than the Cross), *tossed to and fro, and carried about with every wind of doctrine, by the sleight of men*

(Satan uses preachers), *and cunning craftiness* (they make a way, other than the Cross, which seems to be right), *whereby they lie in wait to deceive* (refers to a deliberate planning or system)" (Eph. 4:11-14).

WE BECOME WHAT WE FOLLOW

As is obvious from these texts, not all are called of God. Sadly, some who definitely have been called of God leave the true path of righteousness and go astray. Satan uses many preachers to deceive Christians, and many are successful at what they do.

So, every person must choose carefully the preacher whom they follow. Is he truly preaching the gospel?

If people follow a preacher who is a deceiver, they will become deceivers. If they're following one who is promoting false doctrine in any fashion, they will be deceived by that false doctrine. Conversely, if they are following a preacher who is preaching the truth, the truth will have its positive effect within their lives. So, we'll say it again: every believer should be very careful as to the church they attend and the preacher to whom they listen because of all of the obvious reasons.

Our very souls are at stake!

Elisha would become one of the greatest prophets who ever lived. He didn't, as we shall see, fail the Lord at all. He learned from Elijah and was given that for which he asked, the double portion (II Ki. 2:9), which we will ultimately see.

"Rock of Ages, cleft for me,
"Let me hide myself in Thee;
"Let the water and the blood,
"From Your wounded side which flowed,
"Be of sin the double cure,
"Saved from wrath and make me pure."

"Could my tears forever flow,
"Could my zeal no languor know,
"These for sin could not atone;
"You must save, and You alone;
"In my hand no price I bring,
"Simply to the Cross I cling."

"While I draw this fleeting breath,
"When my eyes shall close in death,
"When I rise to worlds unknown,
"And behold You on Your throne,
"Rock of Ages, cleft for me,
"Let me hide myself in Thee."

ELIJAH
THE TISHBITE

CHAPTER

5

THE UNSCRIPTURAL COVENANT

CHAPTER FIVE

THE UNSCRIPTURAL COVENANT

IN MUCH OF the following material, Elijah is not mentioned, even though he continued to serve as the great prophet to Israel. Yet, I think the Bible student will find tremendous benefit in studying the Israel that existed in Elijah's day. God sent one of the most powerful prophets who ever lived to the northern kingdom of Israel in order to try to stem the tide of sin and shame. Regrettably, it was a hopeless venture. The northern kingdom ultimately went to her doom.

In fact, the entirety of Chapter 20 of I Kings pertains to God's efforts at bringing Israel to a place of repentance. He would allow the threat by the Syrians in its most hateful terms. He would even give Israel a tremendous victory over the Syrians, victories that could be constituted as none other than miracles. Yet, Ahab would not turn away from his wickedness, and Israel would not repent, despite the help the Lord gave them.

Thirty-two kings or vassals, along with all their horses and chariots, were in an alliance with Ben-hadad against Israel.

Ben-hadad was the king of Syria and was a bitter enemy of Israel.

In fact, Syria had been opposed to the people of God from the very beginning. They are opposed presently! In fact, since 1948, Syria has been a leading player in opposing Israel and has been defeated each time.

A PERSONAL EXPERIENCE

If I remember correctly, it was 1986. Israel had long since tired of having rockets rain down on her northern settlements from the Hezbollah in Lebanon and Syria. Therefore, Israel attacked Lebanon with the idea of driving out the Hezbollah, which, in essence, they did.

If the reader can imagine living in a place where rockets sporadically fall upon various settlements, with people constantly being killed and wounded, one can then imagine Israel's position. While the world blamed her for the invasion, the truth is, no civilized government in the world would have put up with it for any length of time, which is what Israel did for several years.

At any rate, I was personally invited by the government of Israel to come to the scene of the conflict and bring our television crew, which we did. We traveled into Beirut, and to be frank, for the first time in my life, I saw the ravages of war up close.

However, the most striking scene we witnessed was certain heights that had been taken by Israel from the Syrians. The battle had only been over for hours when we arrived.

There were dead Syrians everywhere. We walked among the bodies, lives lost in battle. It was a sobering sight! I can well imagine what it must have been like in the heat of battle.

THE REASON FOR THE ANIMOSITY?

The reason for this animosity presently regarding the Syrians against Israel is spiritual. It may be labeled as other things and may be thought of by the world as in other categories; however, pure and simple, it is spiritual.

The animosity of Satan against Israel, and actually against all who believe in the Lord, is evident. Of course, Israel is far away from God, even as she was during the time of Ahab. Still, the Lord has promised by the prophets and by the apostles that Israel will ultimately be restored. This will take place at the second coming; however, until that time, the animosity of the Muslim world against Israel will continue. In fact, this is true for most all the other parts of the world as well. Actually, Israel's darkest days are just ahead. Our Lord called it the *"great tribulation"* (Mat. 24:21), and the great Prophet Jeremiah called it *"the time of Jacob's trouble"* (Jer. 30:7). However, then the prophet said, *"But he shall be saved out of it."* As we have stated, salvation for Israel will come, but it will be by the means of the second coming.

Going back some 2,900 years ago, while conditions were different, the spirit was the same. Inspired by Satan, the Syrians would make every effort to destroy Israel. This time, they would be in for a rude awakening.

THE PROPHET

"And, behold, there came a prophet unto Ahab" (I Ki. 20:13).

Despite the great evil being committed by Israel, the Lord at that time would deem it desirable to deliver His people. Israel belonged to Him, even though most in that nation were far from God.

The message the nameless prophet would bring to Ahab was one of victory for Israel, even though Israel's army was pitifully small and was outnumbered probably 20 or 30 times. This should portray to us the fact that God is not limited or helped by numbers.

The Lord would do all of this for the northern kingdom, showing mercy and grace, all in order to try to bring Israel to her spiritual senses. Unfortunately, all of it was to no avail.

By the prophet coming to Ahab, the king should have known that this conflict was to a far greater degree spiritual rather than anything else. However, Ahab was so dead toward spiritual perception that he was clueless as to what was actually taking place.

As to who exactly this prophet was, the Holy Spirit did not see fit to inform us.

More and more the modern church is pushing away from the things of the Spirit to the things of man. Worse yet, the men to whom it is looking have little true knowledge, if any, of the working of the Holy Spirit. In other words, the modern church is attempting to use the advertising methods of the world. As such, at times it is able to fill the building with warm bodies, but almost no one is truly being born again, much less being baptized with the Holy Spirit, with the latter presently almost non-existent.

As previously stated, the church is supposed to be telling the world how to live, but unfortunately, the world is telling the church instead how to live.

VICTORY!

The prophet of the Lord had told Ahab that he was to first of all send the royal guard against the Syrians. This guard numbered 232 men. Following them would be a small army of some 7,000.

How in the world could this small group defeat the powerful Syrian army, which, as previously stated, outnumbered Israel some 20 or 30 times?

The idea here is not the numbers, but rather obedience to the Word of the Lord. Thankfully, Ahab had enough sense at this time to heed the prophet and to do what he said.

Whenever this small group started out toward the Syrians, Ben-hadad, the Syrian king, told his army to take them alive. (Incidentally, at that moment, Ben-hadad was *"drinking himself drunk."*) I suppose he was speaking of the 232 men, but when the Syrians met these men, they did not exactly find what they had anticipated.

It was as though the 232 men were given supernatural strength, which they, no doubt, had, and, as well, the Syrians were given a spirit of confusion, which they, no doubt, had as well. When the smoke settled and the dust cleared, the Scripture says, as it regards Israel, that they *"killed the Syrians with a great slaughter."* They were able to do that simply because the Lord was with them.

When the Holy Spirit moves, and that's exactly what happened, the natural become supernatural, the weak become strong, the poor become rich, the sick become well, and the small become great.

THE MODERN CHURCH AND THE HOLY SPIRIT

Regrettably and sadly, the church has never been too enamored with the Holy Spirit. At the turn of the 20th century, the latter rain outpouring of the Holy Spirit began, and did so all over the world. It was rejected by virtually the entirety of the church world. It was referred to as *"fanaticism"* or *"ignorance,"* with some even contributing speaking with other tongues to the Devil.

Despite the opposition by the established church, and despite the fact that this small group was basically uneducated, had little or no money, were looked down on and criticized by most of the world, and were even referred to as *"holy rollers,"* they had the one thing that really mattered, the Holy Spirit. By that means, they (we) touched the world, but sadly and regrettably, the role of the Holy Spirit is becoming less and less in far too many modern Pentecostal and charismatic churches. In fact, most of the Pentecostal denominations have opted for the Purpose Driven Life scheme, even though the perpetrator of this claim is not Spirit-filled and does not even believe in it. Of course, in far too many modern so-called Pentecostal churches, being Spirit-filled is no longer a requirement.

Let it be understood that anything and everything truly done for the Lord in this world is always that which is conceived by the Holy Spirit, given birth by the Holy Spirit, empowered by the Holy Spirit, and carried out by the Holy Spirit. Otherwise, it's not of God!

THE BAPTISM WITH THE HOLY SPIRIT

There's a vast difference in being born of the Spirit, which everyone is at conversion, and being baptized with the Spirit. The latter always follows salvation, at least if properly sought (Lk. 11:13).

Concerning this, Jesus said: *"And I will pray the Father, and He shall give you another Comforter* ('Parakletos,' which means 'One called to the side of another to help')*, that He may abide with you forever* (before the Cross, the Holy Spirit could only help a few individuals, and then only for a period of time; since the Cross, He lives in the hearts and lives of all believers, and does so forever);

"Even the Spirit of Truth (the Greek says, 'the Spirit of the Truth,' which refers to the Word of God; actually, He does far more than merely superintend the attribute of Truth, as Christ 'is Truth' [I Jn. 5:6])*; whom the world cannot receive* (the Holy Spirit cannot come into the heart of the unbeliever until that

person makes Christ his or her Saviour; then He comes in), *because it sees Him not, neither knows Him* (refers to the fact that only born-again believers can understand the Holy Spirit and know Him): *but you know Him* (would have been better translated, 'but you shall get to know Him'); *for He dwells with you* (before the Cross), *and shall be in you* (which would take place on the Day of Pentecost and forward, because the sin debt has been forever paid by Christ on the Cross, changing the disposition of everything)" (Jn. 14:16-17).

WHOM THE WORLD CANNOT RECEIVE

If it is to be noticed, our Lord used the phrase, *"whom* (referring to the Holy Spirit) *the world cannot receive."* In other words, it is not possible for an unredeemed person to receive the Holy Spirit. He comes into the heart and the life of a person when the person is born again and not before. However, the baptism with the Spirit can take place seconds after a person is born again, even as it did with Cornelius and those with him (Acts 10:44-48).

So, whenever our non-Pentecostal brethren make their claim that they receive the Holy Spirit at conversion, in a sense, that is certainly true, but what they received was the work of regeneration, carried out by the Holy Spirit. Most definitely He does live in their hearts and lives, and does so with every person who is born again. However, as stated, that is far different than being baptized with the Holy Spirit.

The latter is for power (Acts 1:8) and, as well, for leading and guidance (Jn. 16:13-15).

In fact, the baptism with the Holy Spirit is an experience separate and apart from salvation. In other words, it is received after one is born again, whether immediately or at a later time. Jesus said it is something for which we should ask. He said, *"If you then, being evil, know how to give good gifts unto your children* (means that an earthly parent certainly would not give a child a stone who has asked for bread, etc.)*: how much more shall your heavenly Father give the Holy Spirit to them who ask Him?* (This refers to God's goodness, and the fact that everything from the Godhead comes to us through the person and agency of the Holy Spirit; and all that He does for us is based upon the Cross of Christ and our faith in that finished work.)" (Lk. 11:13).

The baptism with the Holy Spirit does not make one more saved. The moment that one accepts Christ and what He did for us at the Cross, he is just as saved as he will ever be. As stated, the Spirit baptism is for power and service, without which, precious little is going to be done, at least for the Lord.

AN EXPERIENCE SEPARATE FROM SALVATION

There are five accounts given in the book of Acts concerning individuals being baptized with the Holy Spirit. All of these incidents were after the fact, that is, after the fact of salvation.

ACTS 2:4

This account was on the day of Pentecost, which initiated the new dispensation of the Spirit. In other words, the Cross of Christ made all of this possible. We are not told exactly how many were filled that day.

Incidentally, this great occasion took place in the temple, probably in the court of the Gentiles and not in the upper room as many think. While the followers of Christ met in the upper room at different times the previous days, it was in the temple where the Spirit made His great entrance. As should be obvious, all of these people were already saved, i.e., born again.

ACTS 8:14-17

Philip had preached any number of times in Samaria, with many Samaritans being saved; however, none of these individuals were baptized with the Holy Spirit at that time. The Scripture says that when the news about the move of God in Samaria reached the apostles at Jerusalem, *"They sent unto them Peter and John: who, when they were come down, prayed for them, that they might receive the Holy Spirit."*

If individuals are automatically baptized with the Holy Spirit at conversion, as many claim, and there is no experience after salvation, what were Peter and John doing? The answer is simple: They were obeying the Lord. These individuals, although born again, had not yet been baptized with the Spirit. Evidently, Philip did not preach the Spirit baptism to them. Peter and John did, and they did receive.

ACTS 9:17

In the great revelation given to the Apostle Paul on the road to Damascus, the great apostle was saved when he said to the Lord at that moment, *"Lord, what will You have me to do?"* However, he was not baptized with the Holy Spirit at that time, even though, of course, the Holy Spirit most definitely came into his heart and life, as He does with every person who is saved.

The Lord told one of His servants by the name of Ananias to go and pray for Paul to be filled. When he arrived where Paul was staying, He said to him, *"Brother Saul* (his Hebrew name), *the Lord, even Jesus, who appeared unto you in the way as you came, has sent me, that you might receive your sight, and be filled with the Holy Spirit."*

Once again, this proclaims the fact that the Spirit baptism was received some three days after Paul's conversion.

ACTS 10:44-46

The first occasion of the gospel being preached to the Gentiles was done by Simon Peter. The Scripture says that the Holy Spirit suddenly *"fell on all them which heard the Word"* that Peter preached, and Cornelius and all who were with him that day were filled with the Holy Spirit.

These Gentiles were saved, and then moments later, baptized with the Holy Spirit. Remember, Jesus said that the Spirit could not be received until one is first born again (Jn. 14:17).

ACTS 19:1-7

The last account of believers being baptized with the Spirit occurred at Ephesus. Paul arriving there, *"And finding certain disciples, he said unto them, Have you received the Holy Spirit since you believed?"* In the Greek, this is literally, *"Having believed, did you receive?"*

Incidentally, every time the word *disciples* is used in the book of Acts, it refers to individuals who have accepted Christ. Paul could tell that these individuals, although saved, had not yet been baptized with the Holy Spirit.

They confessed to him that they did not understand anything about the Holy Spirit, at least that of which he was speaking.

Paul evidently explained this to them and then *"laid his hands upon them."* When he did this, they were baptized with the Holy Spirit.

The idea of my correlation of events is as follows:

- While one most definitely does receive the Holy Spirit at conversion, this is the Spirit of regeneration. The baptism with the Spirit follows, that is, if the believer asks for this experience.

- There is a vast difference in being born of the Spirit, which everyone is at salvation, than being baptized with the Spirit.
- Being baptized with the Spirit does not make one more saved. The moment one accepts Christ, he or she is just as saved as he will ever be. The baptism with the Spirit is for power and service.
- We believe the Bible teaches (the proof of which we have given in the preceding paragraphs) that the baptism with the Spirit is a definite, distinct experience that is received after salvation, which is available to every believer.
- We believe also that every believer, with no exception, speaks with other tongues the moment he or she is baptized with the Spirit.

TONGUES AS THE INITIAL PHYSICAL EVIDENCE

We believe the Bible teaches that speaking with other tongues is the initial, physical evidence that one has been baptized with the Holy Spirit. There are no exceptions to this. In other words, it's not possible to be baptized with the Holy Spirit without speaking with other tongues.

Once again, looking at the five accounts of believers being baptized with the Spirit, we will see that speaking with other tongues is the initial, physical evidence that one has received.

THE DAY OF PENTECOST

The Scripture says, and I quote from The Expositor's Study Bible:

"And they were all filled with the Holy Spirit (all were filled, not just the apostles; due to the Cross, the Holy Spirit could now come into the hearts and lives of all believers to abide permanently [Jn. 14:16]), *and began to speak with other tongues* (the initial physical evidence, as stated, that one has been baptized with the Spirit, and was predicted by the Prophet Isaiah [Isa. 28:9-12], and by Christ [Mk. 16:17; Jn. 15:26; 16:13]), *as the Spirit gave them utterance* (meaning they did not initiate this themselves, but that it was initiated by the Spirit; as we shall see, these were languages known somewhere in the world, but not by the speaker)" (Acts 2:4).

THE SAMARITANS

The second occasion pertains to the Samaritans, who had been saved under the ministry of Philip. Peter and John came and preached to these individuals and then *"prayed for them, that they might receive the Holy Spirit."*

The Scripture doesn't tell us what happened; it merely says that they received.

However, when Simon the sorcerer tried to purchase this gift from Peter as this man saw the individuals baptized with the Spirit, Peter said to him, *"Your money perish with you, because you have thought that the gift of God may be purchased with money."*

He then said, *"You have neither part nor lot in this matter."* The word *matter* in the Greek, as it is used here, is *logos* and means *"a word or speech."* Peter was referring to these believers speaking with other tongues (Acts 8:18-21).

PAUL

Again, when Paul was filled with the Spirit, the Bible gives us no information at all as to what happened. It just merely stated in the words of Ananias, *"That you might receive your sight, and be filled with the Holy Spirit."*

Yet, concerning speaking with tongues, the Apostle Paul himself said, *"I thank my God, I speak with tongues more than you all"* (I Cor. 14:18).

No, Paul was not speaking of his linguistic abilities, referring to his ability to speak several languages, but rather of glossolalia. In fact, the entirety of Chapter 14 of I Corinthians deals with this very subject, even as given by Paul.

CORNELIUS AND HIS HOUSEHOLD

The fourth occasion concerns Cornelius and his household and Peter preaching to them. The Scripture says, *"And they of the circumcision* (Jews) *which believed* (believed in Christ) *were astonished* (at what they saw the Lord doing, which could not be denied), *as many as came with Peter, because that on*

the Gentiles also was poured out the gift of the Holy Spirit
(Cornelius and his household were saved, and then moments
later baptized with the Holy Spirit; it was quite a meeting!).

"*For they heard them speak with tongues* (this is the initial, physical evidence that one has been baptized with the
Holy Spirit; it always and without exception accompanies
the Spirit baptism), *and magnify God* (means that some of
them would stop speaking in tongues momentarily and then
begin to praise God in their natural language, magnifying
His name)" (Acts 10:45-46).

THE EPHESIAN DISCIPLES

The last account is given of the disciples at Ephesus. Paul
ascertained that these men, although saved, had not yet been
baptized with the Holy Spirit.

The Scripture says, "*And when Paul had laid his hands
upon them* (constitutes a biblical principle [Acts 8:17; 9:17-
18]), *the Holy Spirit came on them* (refers to them being
baptized with the Holy Spirit); *and they spoke with tongues,
and prophesied* (proclaims tongues as the initial physical
evidence that one has been baptized with the Holy Spirit;
sometimes there is prophesying at that time, and sometimes
not [Acts 8:17; 9:17; 10:46])" (Acts 19:1-7).

I think the Scripture is replete with the evidence that
speaking with other tongues always accompanies the baptism with the Holy Spirit. As previously stated, there are no

exceptions. They are languages known somewhere in the world but not by the one who has been baptized with the Spirit (Acts 2:7-11).

THE VALUE OF TONGUES

- First of all, tongues are a proclamation of *"the wonderful works of God"* (Acts 2:11).
- Tongues are the utterance instigated by the Holy Spirit (Acts 2:4).
- Tongues are that which was predicted by the prophets Joel and Isaiah (Joel 2:28; Isa. 28:11).
- Tongues are a promise given by God (Acts 2:17).
- Tongues magnify God (Acts 10:46).
- Tongues *"speak not unto men, but unto God"* (I Cor. 14:2).
- Tongues edify the believer, which, at times, is desperately needed (I Cor. 14:4).
- When one prays in tongues, one's spirit prays, which is a higher form of prayer than that which comes from the mind (I Cor. 14:14).
- Tongues are for a sign, not to them who believe, but to them who believe not (I Cor. 14:22).
- Speaking in tongues brings about rest for the child of God. The Scripture says, *"This is the rest wherewith you may cause the weary to rest"* (Isa. 28:12).
- Tongues are also a *"refreshing"* (Isa. 28:12).

Once again, the strength of the church is the Holy Spirit. To be sure, the Holy Spirit will always glorify Christ and what He has done for us at the Cross (Jn. 16:14-15).

THE PROPHET

The Scripture says, *"And the prophet came to the king of Israel, and said unto him, Go, strengthen yourself, and mark, and see what you do: for at the return of the year the king of Syria will come up against you"* (I Ki. 20:22).

The prophet here mentioned is not Elijah. Actually, he is not identified in Scripture.

The Syrians recognized that it was God who had defeated them, but they looked at Jehovah as a local deity and, in this case, a god of the hills. So, if they fought in the valley, the God of Israel would be helpless, or so they thought. Unredeemed man has no idea of who God is, or what God is!

With the help of the Lord, which was by the power of God, Israel won a tremendous victory, killing some 100,000 Syrians in one day.

Whether the man of God of Verse 28 was the same person as the prophet of Verse 22 is not quite clear. This was being done by the Lord for Israel for their benefit, but also, that neighboring nations might learn His power and that His name might be magnified among them.

THE POWER OF GOD

"And the servants of the king of Syria said unto him, Their gods are gods of the hills; therefore they were stronger than we; but let us fight against them in the plain, and surely we shall be stronger than they" (I Ki. 20:23).

Verse 23 proclaims the worship of heathen gods by the Syrians. Every heathen country of that time attributed their military and economic success to their god. They had reason, as stated, *"Their gods are gods of the hills."* So, now they would fight in the valley, and supposedly, their god would be stronger than Israel's God.

The spiritual situation has changed little from that day until now. The whole world witnessed the demise of atheistic communism in 1989. They had proclaimed *"no God,"* and God called them *"a fool"* (Ps. 14:1).

Look at the part of the world that is ruled by satanic Hinduism. It is steeped in ignorance, superstition, and poverty. The same can be said for Buddhism.

Most of Africa, sadly and regrettably, is ruled by witchcraft, Islam, and Catholicism. In fact, despite the boasts of Christendom concerning the evangelization of Africa, only a small part of the continent of Africa can accurately be said to be Christian. Africa suffers accordingly.

The world of Islam controls nearly 1 billion human beings. It substitutes the Koran for the Bible. It is a false book with a false message, as its prophet Muhammad was a false prophet.

Islam is the instigator of virtually all of the terrorism in the world today. They function on the premise of hate.

Its prosperity, at least what little it has, comes from American money for Islamic oil. It is advancing, sad to say, at a fearful rate, evangelizing the world by force and by money. The religion of Islam could very well have a great part to play in the coming great tribulation and the rise of the Antichrist.

THE GOD OF THE BIBLE

Much of Central and South America is ruled by superstitious Catholicism and, thereby, worships a god that does not exist, namely the Virgin Mary.

Christianity definitely is making some inroads into Latin America but still has much ground to cover.

The point is this: The God of the Bible is the bringer of all blessing and salvation. There is no other. Sadly, most of the world worships demon spirits in one form or the other. Correspondingly, most of the world is steeped in superstition, heathenism, abject poverty, and slavery. America and Canada, along with England and a few other countries, have experienced many blessings because of biblical Christianity. Regrettably, anymore, these nations little recognize or understand the source of their blessing. They attribute such to their educational processes, secular humanism, or to their own prideful selves. In many nations of the world, true biblical Christianity has never been weaker; consequently, the fountain of light that has been provided to a lost world is dimmer today, I think, than ever before, at least since the Reformation.

At this time, England is boasting of a *"spiritual renaissance."* What do they call a spiritual renaissance?

A SPIRITUAL RENAISSANCE?

The Anglican priests in the Church of England are using the Koran at least once a month in their services. How the mighty have fallen. America is little, if any, better. In the public school systems of this nation and other public institutions, neither God nor the Lord Jesus Christ can be mentioned under the guise of the separation of church and state. The truth is, it's a separation of God and state.

We are quickly becoming a secular, humanistic, and atheistic nation. We are forgetting the fact that there is no light but the light of the gospel. There is no true education but the education of the Word of God. There is no blessing apart from God.

Sadly, America and Canada, as well as the other nations of the world that espouse Christianity, are little better, if any at all, than the Israel of Ahab's day. God is still helping us, but how long will He do so with our present spiritual state?

Because the Lord was with Israel despite her spiritual declension, Israel would see a tremendous victory over the Syrians, in fact, a victory of unprecedented proportions.

THE UNSCRIPTURAL COVENANT

Ahab took a most ridiculous position as it regarded his attitude toward Ben-hadad, who, as is obvious, was trying to kill him. What Ahab did was greatly displeasing to the Lord.

What should Ahab have done as it regarded Ben-hadad?

He should have executed him on the spot.

Despite the fact that the Lord had been so good to Ahab, he had no relationship whatsoever with the Lord. In a sense, he was more in tune with Ben-hadad than he was the ways of the Lord. Seemingly, he didn't have enough sense to realize what his actions would bring forth. Because of his failure to obey the Lord, Syria would once again be a threat to Israel, and a great threat at that! In fact, this same Syrian king with which he had made an ill-advised covenant would kill him about four years later.

Instead, the Scripture says, *"And Ben-hadad said unto him, The cities, which my father took from your father, I will restore; and you shall make streets for you in Damascus, as my father made in Samaria. Then said Ahab, I will send you away with this covenant. So he made a covenant with him, and sent him away"* (I Ki. 20:34).

The child of God must have no truck with the world. While we are in the world, we most definitely must never be of the world. Ultimately, it will turn and bite us, even as it did Ahab of so long ago.

THE WORD OF THE LORD

"And he (the prophet) *said unto him* (said to Ahab), *Thus says the* LORD, *Because you* (Ahab) *have let go out of your hand a man whom I appointed to utter destruction* (Ben-hadad), *therefore your life shall go for his life, and your people for his people"* (I Ki. 20:42).

Ahab had seriously displeased the Lord in letting Ben-hadad go free. He would now pay the price, even though it would be several years in coming.

Ahab most assuredly had known what the Lord intended to do with Ben-hadad; therefore, he clearly ignored what the Lord desired, which would ultimately result in the loss of his life.

As it regarded Syria, all of this was the word of the Lord and most definitely meant to be obeyed. It is no different presently.

The Bible, the word of the Lord, is meant to be the criterion, the final word on everything. In fact, there is nothing in the world more important than the Word of God.

THE BIBLE

The reader must understand that the Bible is not merely a collection of men's ideas and thoughts, as holy and godly as they may have been. The Bible was given to us as the Holy Spirit moved upon the particular writers, even choosing the very words that God desired to be used. So, what we read in the King James Version of the Bible and in one or two other word-for-word translations is the word of the Lord. This means it is inviolable. It is not to be ignored, deleted, or added to. Also, believers should seek to understand it, thereby, studying it daily and asking the Lord for understanding, leading, and guidance, which He will most assuredly give.

That's the reason that we urge all believers to avail themselves of The Expositor's Study Bible. I personally believe that there is no study Bible in the world today that can help one understand the Word of God more than The Expositor's Study Bible. As well, it is the most user-friendly Bible that one could ever begin to use.

Ahab ignored the word of the Lord, and it cost him his life and his soul. It is no less severe presently. If we ignore the word of the Lord, our fate in some way will be the same as his.

"Jesus has loved me, wonderful Saviour!
"Jesus has loved me, I cannot tell why;
"Came He to rescue sinners all worthless,
"My heart He conquered, for Him I would die."

"Jesus has saved me, wonderful Saviour!
"Jesus has saved me, I cannot tell how;
"All that I know is He was my ransom,
"Dying on Calvary with thorns on His brow."

"Jesus will lead me, wonderful Saviour!
"Jesus will lead me, I cannot tell where;
"But I will follow, through joy or sorrow,
"Sunshine or tempest, sweet peace or despair."

"Jesus will crown me, wonderful Saviour!
"Jesus will crown me, I cannot tell when;
"White throne of splendor hail I with gladness,
"Crowned 'mid the plaudits of angels and men."

ELIJAH
THE TISHBITE

CHAPTER

6

THE VINEYARD

CHAPTER SIX

THE VINEYARD

"AND IT CAME to pass after these things, that Naboth the Jezreelite had a vineyard, which was in Jezreel, hard by the palace of Ahab king of Samaria" (I Ki. 21:1).

The entirety of this chapter concerns the vineyard. Naboth's vineyard is a type of the spiritual inheritance that every child of God has. As his vineyard bordered Ahab's palace, so our spiritual inheritance (vineyard) borders the world.

The same pressure that was applied by Ahab against Naboth to sell his vineyard will be applied to us by the forces of darkness to compromise our convictions. As the battle was to the death, so will the battle that we fight be unto the death. We have but one of two choices:

1. We can refuse Satan any part in that which God has given us.
2. We can sell out to Ahab (the world).

The first one will bring physical death but spiritual life. The second one will bring physical life but spiritual death.

Satan professes to have better vineyards, but he lies. If he has better vineyards, why does he want yours?

As Naboth's vineyard was given unto him by the Lord of glory, likewise, our vineyard of salvation is given to us by the Lord of glory.

Actually, the law of Moses forbade the sale of ancestral rights except in extreme destitution, and even then, the property would always return to the original owners in the Year of Jubilee (Lev. 25:23-25; Num. 36:7).

THE VINEYARD

Strangely enough, in some ways, Ahab was a great king as the world goes, at least as far as his public works and palaces testify. He was a gifted and able prince and far surpassed other kings of Israel in the energy, culture, and splendor of his reign. Yet, the Word of God says that he was wicked beyond compare.

Verse 1 says, *"That Naboth the Jezreelite had a vineyard."* As stated, the entirety of this chapter concerns this vineyard. The Scripture further says it was *"hard by the palace of Ahab king of Samaria."*

The account of this vineyard characterizes two principles regarding the Word of God.

1. Naboth was a type of Christ cast out of the vineyard (Mat. 21:39). In this case, Ahab is seen as the Israel who murdered Christ.

2. Naboth's vineyard is a type of the spiritual inheritance that every child of God actually has. The same pressure that was applied by Ahab against Naboth to sell his vineyard will be applied to us by the forces of darkness to compromise our convictions. As this battle was to the death, so will the battle that we fight be unto the death.

Verse 2 says of Ahab as he speaks to Naboth, *"Give me your vineyard, that I may have it for a garden of herbs."* Ahab's offer would be in two directions.

A BETTER VINEYARD?

Ahab proposed to give to Naboth a better vineyard for his vineyard. If his was better, why did he want that which belonged to Naboth?

Satan professes to have better vineyards, but he lies. If he has better vineyards, why does he want yours? The truth is, he doesn't have a better vineyard. In fact, Satan's vineyards are of no comparison to those of the Lord's. That's the reason he wants yours.

AHAB OFFERED TO BUY IT FOR MONEY

To be sure, the temptation to sell out for personal gain is powerful, and many are yielding to it. However, Simon Peter wrote that our redemption was not purchased with such corruptible things as silver and gold but with the precious blood of Jesus (I Pet. 1:18-19). So, money cannot buy this vineyard, yet Satan probably has more success with this offer than anything else. The Holy Spirit was once the driving force of the church, at least for those who truly wanted God. Presently, all too often the driving force is money.

THE LAW OF MOSES

Actually, the law of Moses, as stated, forbade the sale of ancestral rights except in extreme destitution, and even then, the property would have to return to the original owners in the year of release (Lev. 25:23-25; Num. 36:7).

In those days, such inheritances from forefathers, which had been passed on for many generations in the same family, were considered priceless, and to part with such was almost like parting with life itself. The reason was obvious: it was given by God and had very dear associations connected with it concerning one's ancestors.

As it concerns that which the Lord has given us, the answer for every child of God must be the same as Naboth's, *"The Lord forbid it me."* Satan will ever try to take our vineyard. He must be repulsed even unto the death.

TOUCH NOT THE LORD'S ANOINTED

"And it came to pass, when Jezebel heard that Naboth was stoned, and was dead, that Jezebel said to Ahab, Arise, take possession of the vineyard of Naboth the Jezreelite,

which he refused to give you for money: for Naboth is not alive, but dead" (I Ki. 21:15).

Jezebel would take the vineyard by brute force. Actually, this idol-worshipping murderer would take the life of this man of God. She wrote a letter to the elders of Samaria, in effect, leaving the impression that the city was laboring under or threatened with a curse because of some undiscovered sin. It had to be removed or averted by public humiliation.

In this gathering, Naboth, at Jezebel's command, was assigned the most distinguished place. All of this was a part of the ploy.

She would have two men, worthless individuals, to accuse Naboth of blaspheming. Stoning was the legal punishment for blasphemy. There were no accusers of Naboth other than these two worthless sons of the Devil, whomever they may have been. Upon their word, the crowd *"stoned him* (Naboth) *with stones, that he died."* Now Ahab could take the vineyard and wouldn't have to pay anything for it.

According to Pulpit, there is a proud, malicious triumph in the words, *"He refused, simple fool, to sell it. Now you can have it for nothing."*

THE WAYS OF THE LORD

Of course, the Lord could have easily stopped this insidious plan against Naboth. He did not do so for His own reasons. He allowed this true follower of the Lord to be killed in a most terrible way.

Why?

The Lord evidently deemed that the death of Naboth would suffer him better than for him to continue to live. Some years later, the great Prophet Isaiah would say: *"The righteous perish and no man lays it to heart: and merciful men are taken away, none considering that the righteous is taken away from the evil to come"* (Isa. 57:1).

The word translated *perish* does not necessarily imply violence, but the context implies a premature death. The righteous disappear—are taken from the earth before their natural time.

The text is so structured that, in effect, the Holy Spirit is saying that these *"righteous"* were not appreciated, but rather hated for their godly walk. As such, they were a rebuke to ungodly but religious Israel, and the Lord prematurely took them away in death. The phrase, *"No man lays it to heart,"* refers to the fact that no one asked what it meant, no one was disturbed, and no one grieved, which means that no one cared.

"And merciful men are taken away," implies that mercy was found only in these few righteous. When these were taken, in this case, only one, Naboth, very little mercy was left in the religious heart of a spiritually demented Israel!

The phrase, *"None considering that the righteous is taken away from the evil to come,"* refers to the fact that God may permit the premature death of His servants as an escape from calamities worse than death.

While the words of Isaiah 57:1 had not yet been written, still, they were in the mind of God. This was, no doubt, the reason that God allowed Naboth to be killed at that time. The Lord looked at Israel as an unfit place for the godly to dwell. So, He took Naboth away.

THE JUDGMENT OF GOD

"And the Word of the LORD *came to Elijah the Tishbite, saying"* (I Ki. 21:17).

As the word of the Lord through the Prophet Elijah was given to Ahab, the words of Jesus come to mind: *"With what measure you mete, it shall be measured to you again"* (Mat. 7:2). This chapter opens with Ahab refusing to listen to God's loving voice, which was spoken to him so plainly in the remarkable victory given to him over the Syrians. Instead, he willingly listened to Jezebel's cruel voice, which was prompting him to commit perhaps the blackest of his black crimes — Naboth.

In fact, the terrible judgment pronounced upon Jezebel by Elijah proclaimed the fact that retribution should overtake her near the scene of her latest crime. It would be recorded in II Kings 9:36. By this, the just judgment of God would be made the more conspicuous.

Ahab was the most wicked king of Israel thus far, and, in fact, this program of ever-increasing wickedness continued until the whole nation had to be destroyed.

THE WORD OF THE LORD

As stated, Verse 17 says, *"The word of the LORD came to Elijah the Tishbite, saying."* To be sure, this word would be severe. In effect, it says, *"What you sow you will reap."*

It should ever be understood that this is an unbreakable law with God. The only thing that can abate this stern judgment is sincere repentance. The Lord Jesus Himself taught, *"With what measure you mete, it shall be measured to you again"* (Mat. 7:2). The pronouncement of doom would be on both Ahab and Jezebel.

In all of their wickedness, when they touched the Lord's anointed, they, in effect, touched the Lord in a most derogatory manner.

Verse 25 states, *"But there was none like unto Ahab, which did sell himself to work wickedness in the sight of the LORD, whom Jezebel his wife stirred up."*

AHAB

Ahab was the most wicked king of Israel thus far. The wickedness of the kings of the northern kingdom was increasing despite the judgments of God. It was said of Jeroboam, the first king of the Ten Tribes, that he turned not from his evil and that he laid the foundation of sin for all his people (I Ki. 13:33-34). It was said of Nadab, Baasha, and Elah, the second, third, and fourth kings of the Ten Tribes, that they walked in the way of Jeroboam and of Omri. It is said that he did worse than all the kings before him, and now, it is said of Ahab that there was none like him thus far. This program of ever-increasing wickedness continued until the entire nation had to be destroyed.

The thoughts of man's heart toward God are thoughts of unbelief, rebellion, and hatred, while the thoughts of God's heart toward man are thoughts of pity and love.

What Ahab had (Ben-hadad of the last chapter), he let go, and what he had not (the vineyard), he coveted. Such is the heart of the unspiritual man.

Could the judgment of God pronounced on both Ahab and Jezebel have been avoided had they truly repented?

Yes!

While there would have been some suffering, still, the awful doom pronounced would have been avoided.

In fact, Ahab would repent, even as we shall see, but only after a fashion. Even then, the Lord showed him mercy!

THE MODERN CHURCH AND THE JUDGMENT OF GOD

The judgment of God upon sin is rarely mentioned anymore from behind modern pulpits. The modern message actually comes in twin forms. They are: the morality message and the motivation message.

THE MORALITY MESSAGE

This message constantly tells mankind how to be better and how to do better, which sounds good to the ear of man, for most desire to be morally better. However, let it be understood that that which God demands of human beings cannot be brought about by a man, no matter the schemes concocted, etc. It can only be brought about by the Holy Spirit.

In other words, the Holy Spirit alone can make us holy, make us righteous, and rid all sin out of our lives, at least dominating sin. Man through his own ingenuity, ability, personal strength, and efforts cannot bring these things to pass. In fact, in that fashion, such is impossible.

The Holy Spirit works entirely within the framework of the Cross of Christ. In other words, it is the atoning work carried out by Christ on the Cross that gives the Holy Spirit the legal right to do what He needs to do within our hearts and lives (Rom. 8:2). It is only demanded of us, at least the part we are to play, that our faith be anchored firmly in Christ and the Cross (Rom. 6:1-14; 8:1-11; I Cor. 1:17-18, 23; 2:2; Gal. 6:14; Col. 2:10-15). Faith properly placed and faith properly maintained will guarantee the help of the Holy Spirit, with the attributes of the fruit of the Spirit then brought about within our lives. It can be done no other way.

THE MOTIVATION MESSAGE

The prideful heart of man loves to be stroked. The modern message does just that. It tells man how that he in reality is a champion, and if he will do certain things, the champion that is within him will be brought out. He is told how great and wonderful he is, which sounds good to the modern ear. The truth is, the Scripture says something entirely opposite.

What it does say is: *"As it is written* (Ps. 14:1-3), *There is none righteous, no, not one:*

"There is none who understands (proclaims total depravity), *there is none who seek after God* (man left on his own will not seek God and, in fact, cannot seek God; he is spiritually dead).

"They are all gone out of the way (speaks of the lost condition of men; the 'way' is God's way), *they are together become unprofitable* (refers to the terrible loss in every capacity of wayward man); *there is none who does good, no, not one* (the Greek text says, 'useless!').

"Their throat is an open sepulchre (the idea is of an open grave, with the rotting remains sending forth a putrid stench); *with their tongues they have used deceit* (speaks of guile, deception, hypocrisy, etc.); *the poison of asps is under their lips* (man cannot be trusted in anything he says)*:*

"Whose mouth is full of cursing (wishing someone evil or hurt) *and bitterness* (bitter and reproachful language)*:*

"Their feet are swift to shed blood (the world is filled with murder, killing, and violence)*:*

"Destruction and misery are in their ways (all brought about by sin)*:*

"And the way of peace have they not known (and cannot know until Christ returns)*:*

"There is no fear of God before their eyes (there is no fear of God because unbelieving man does not know God)" (Rom. 3:10-18).

HUMANISTIC PSYCHOLOGY

That which we have just given is what God says that man actually is, which is a far cry from the prattle of the modern pulpit. In fact, most churches look to humanistic psychology, which, in essence, denies everything that Paul wrote in Chapter 3 of Romans. How is it that preachers can claim to believe the Bible and at the same time embrace that which is 180 degrees removed from the Word of God?

In such a climate, sin is not mentioned, man's depravity is not mentioned, and above all, the judgment of God is not mentioned because it may offend man. So, instead, he is fed spiritual cotton candy on an unending basis. The end result is obvious!

Irrespective of all this, God's judgment against sin is just as strong today as it was when Elijah the Tishbite pronounced doom upon both Ahab and Jezebel. In fact, the Cross of Christ alone is the only thing that stands between mankind and eternal death. However, if men reject the Cross and will not accept what Jesus did there, nothing is left but judgment.

DOESN'T THE DISPENSATION OF GRACE SET ASIDE THE JUDGMENT OF GOD?

No!

The judgment of God in this dispensation of grace is even greater than it was under law.

Listen to the Word of God. Paul said, *"Forasmuch then as we are the offspring of God* (is offered by Paul in the sense of creation; it does not mean the 'fatherhood of God and the brotherhood of man,' as many contend)*, we ought not to think that the Godhead is like unto gold, or silver, or stone, graven by art and man's device* (Paul is saying that God is not a device of man, as all the Greek gods in fact were).

"And the times of this ignorance God winked at (does not reflect that such ignorance was salvation, for it was not! before the Cross, there was very little light in the world, so God withheld judgment)*; but now commands all men everywhere to repent* (but since the Cross, the 'way' is open to all; it's up to us believers to make that 'way' known to all men)" (Acts 17:29-30).

From this passage, one can say that there is far more judgment (which comes in all forms) evidenced in the world presently than there was under the old law or anytime before the Cross.

The grace of God, which is actually the goodness of God extended to undeserving men, is simply that the Cross has made it easier for men to approach the Lord. It does not give men a license to sin, and it does not mean that God abates judgment, in other words, that He winks at sin. He never has, and He never will!

While judgment does not always come at the moment of sin, to be sure, barring repentance, it will ultimately come.

THE CROSS OF CHRIST

In Old Testament times, Israel constituted the only people on earth who knew anything at all about the Lord. Sadly, only a few Israelites at any one time actually lived for God. This means that Israel was the only monotheistic people on the face of the earth, meaning that they served one God, Jehovah, at least the few who did. Every other nation in the world was polytheistic, meaning they served many gods, actually demon spirits. All of this means that there was very little light in the world.

The Lord intended for Israel to evangelize the world, but regrettably, Israel became very sectarian and drew in upon themselves, actually hating all Gentiles.

However, now that the Cross is a fact, the gospel of Christ has spread out all over the world. At the time of this writing, this particular ministry (Jimmy Swaggart Ministries) reaches approximately 1 billion people due to television and the Internet. Of course, only a tiny fraction of that number of people actually watch the programming, but it is available to all the others if they so desire.

The fact is, the judgment of God was poured out upon God's Son, the Lord Jesus Christ, while He was on the Cross of Calvary. This was judgment for sin that should have come upon us, but which our Lord instead took the fatal blow. All of this was planned from before the foundation of the world. God through foreknowledge knew that man, His choice creation, would fall. It was then determined by the Godhead that God would become man and, thereby, go to the Cross so that the price would be paid, which would satisfy the demands of a thrice-holy God. Jesus did not go to the Cross to satisfy Satan; He went there to satisfy God. On the Cross, He atoned for all sin — past, present, and future — at least for all who will believe (Jn. 3:16). By Christ atoning for all sin, it removed the legal right that Satan had to hold man captive. Therefore, the only reason that he can hold man captive today, which he does, is because unredeemed man will not accept Jesus Christ. Sadly, most Christians are ruled by the sin nature simply because they do not know or understand God's prescribed order of victory for life and living. So, as stated, they are ruled by the sin nature, which makes life miserable.

The following must be understood:

- Jesus Christ is the source of all the wonderful things we receive from God (Jn. 1:1-3, 14, 29; 14:6; Col. 2:10-15).
- The Cross of Christ is the means and the only means by which all of these wonderful things can come to us (Rom. 6:1-14; I Cor. 1:17-18, 23; 2:2).
- With Jesus Christ being the source and the Cross being the means, the object of our faith without fail must be in Christ and the Cross. In fact, *"Jesus Christ and*

Him crucified" is the entirety of the story of the Bible (Jn. 3:16; Col. 2:10-15).

- If we are functioning in the capacity just mentioned, the Holy Spirit, who works exclusively within the framework of the Cross of Christ, will then work mightily on our behalf, giving us victory over the world, the flesh, and the Devil. While the Bible does not teach sinless perfection, it most definitely does teach that sin is not to have dominion over us. If we follow these guidelines, we can walk in victory and supremely enjoy that for which Jesus has paid such a price (Rom. 8:1-11; Eph. 2:13-18).

The grace of God, which is actually the goodness of God extended to undeserving people, is simply that the Cross has made it easier for men to approach the Lord. It does not give men a license to sin, and it does not mean that God abates judgment, in other words, that He winks at sin. He never has, and He never will!

While judgment does not always come at the moment of sin, to be sure, barring repentance, it will ultimately come.

Please understand that the only thing standing between man and eternal hell is the Cross of Christ.

REPENTANCE

It seems that Ahab's repentance was sincere, at least for a time. God would not have spoken to a half-hearted repentance.

Regarding the prediction of judgment coming upon Ahab's son, there is no threat of punishment here against the innocent instead of the guilty, as might appear at first sight. In the first place, God knew well what the son would be, and in the second place, if the son had departed from his father's sins, he would have been spared as well (Ezek. 18:14).

Judgment was deferred to give the house of Ahab another chance but, regrettably, to no avail!

In this scenario, one can easily see that for which God asks and actually demands — humility.

Repentance is seldom engaged by the church simply because it is an ugly business. One has to admit wrongdoing. It seems that only the most destitute can do so.

Of the myriad man-made offices so predominant in the modern church, one almost never hears of repentance from those who occupy these man-made positions.

Why?

PRIDE DOES NOT LEND ITSELF TOWARD REPENTANCE

For the most part, the religious positions mentioned, of whatever capacity, are man-devised and, thereby, unscriptural. To play the political game in order to occupy one of these offices invariably precludes any type of humility. With some few exceptions, only those who would desire such positions do so because of pride. Consequently, pride does not lend itself toward repentance.

Actually, at this particular time, repentance is such a rarity in the modern church that the church really does not even know what to do with one who repents. Due to a plethora of man-made rules, repentance toward God is not even recognized, only repentance toward man. God will not accept repentance toward man simply because it is God who has been offended by our sin. There is not a single Christian denomination in America and Canada, at least of which I am aware, that will accept repentance toward God. Every single one, again, of which I am aware, completely ignores the Word of God and makes up its own rules, which by and large deny repentance. Repentance is always toward God and never toward man. While it certainly may be true that repentance toward God may include the asking of forgiveness of man, still, all sin is, in its conception, directed toward God.

GOD'S FORGIVENESS

If one will notice, Ahab, who was one of the most wicked men who ever lived, repented instantly, and God forgave instantly. Repentance is admitting the wrong, condemning oneself, and totally justifying God. It is completely turning around from the erroneous direction that one has been traveling. So, Ahab, at least for a short period of time, turned away from the devilish path that he had previously been traveling. The Lord would hear and would show mercy!

However, sadly, even as we shall see, the repentance of this man was of short duration. In other words, he quickly succumbed back to the old way.

PSALM 51

Psalm 51 is a psalm of David written when Nathan the prophet came unto him after the sin with Bath-sheba and the murder of her husband Uriah (II Sam., Chpt. 12). This psalm was given by the Holy Spirit to David when his heart was broken and contrite because of his sin. He pleaded with God for pardon through the atoning blood of the Lamb of God, foreshadowed in Exodus, Chapter 12. Thus, he was not only fittingly provided with a vehicle of expression in repentance and faith, but he was also used as a channel of prophetic communication.

David, in his sin, repentance, and restoration, is also a forepicture of Israel. As he forsook the law and was guilty of adultery and murder, so Israel despised the covenant, turned aside to idolatry (spiritual adultery), and murdered the Messiah.

Thus the scope and structure of this psalm goes far beyond David. It predicts the future confession and forgiveness of Israel in the day of the Messiah's second coming, when looking upon Him whom they pierced, they shall mourn and weep (Zech., Chpts. 12-13).

As well, this is even more perfectly a vivid portrayal of the intercessory work of Christ on behalf of His people. Even though David prayed this prayer, the Son of David would make David's sin (as well as ours) His own and pray through him that which must be said.

This means that this is the truest prayer of repentance ever prayed because it symbolizes the intercessory work of the Son of David.

CONFESSION OF SIN

There is a teaching that is becoming quite dominant in this country and elsewhere. In essence, it claims that the Cross of Christ addressed all sin — past, present, and future — which is exactly correct. Most definitely the Cross did do this. However, then it states that with this being the case, when a Christian sins, the believer does not have to confess his sin, ask forgiveness, or even mention it at all because all future sins have been atoned, as well. In other words, just go on as if nothing has ever happened. Plain and simple, this is error. As all error does, sooner or later it will cause the believer terrible problems. In fact, some will even lose their souls.

TRUTH AND ERROR

One of Satan's chief ploys is to mix some truth in with error. The truth serves as bait, with the believer then thinking that all that is said must be correct. So, the fact that error contains some truth doesn't make it acceptable at all. The believer has to listen very carefully to what he is hearing. To be sure, the idea that a Christian doesn't need to confess his sin to the Lord whenever sin is committed is facetious indeed!

ALL SIN IS AGAINST GOD

The believer must understand the truth of our heading in that all sin is ultimately against God. Considering that when we sin, we have offended Him, it means that we have to ask forgiveness for that sin. If a husband wrongs his wife, he must go to his wife, ask her forgiveness, and admit that he was wrong, that is, if he was. With that failing to be done, the relationship in that marriage will begin to weaken. It is the same with the Lord.

WHAT HAPPENS TO A CHRISTIAN WHO BELIEVES THIS LIE?

What we're asking concerns the believer who believes this error and never asks forgiveness for anything that he's done that's wrong. What will be the results?

God is patient, loving, and kind. He doesn't throw us over when we make a mistake or when we do something foolish. He seeks to bring us back to the fold. However, when one fails the Lord in any capacity, even in the act of refusing to confess our sin to Him, relationship is somewhat hindered. It cannot be otherwise. God is the judge; however, if the believer continues on that erroneous path, there will come a time that the wrong direction will reap its results, and it won't be pretty.

WHAT DOES THE BIBLE SAY?

John said, *"If we confess our sins, He is faithful and just to forgive us our sins, and to cleanse us from all unrighteousness"* (I Jn. 1:9).

The purveyors of the false doctrine which opposes confession claim that this passage is to the unsaved world and not believers.

This is basely incorrect. A cursory glimpse of Chapter 1 of the epistle of I John completely refutes such erroneous thinking. In the first place, an unsaved person cannot confess his sins to the Lord, for they are too many. While he can confess that he is a sinner, that's all he can do. However, John here told us to *"confess our sins."*

HOW IS CONFESSION TO BE DONE?

The Lord has made it simple and easy. To confess wrongdoing to the Lord, one doesn't have to go to church, call a preacher, etc. From his heart, even silently if he so desires, he simply should tell the Lord that he has done wrong and ask for mercy and grace, which the Lord will always provide.

Those who teach this erroneous doctrine of anti-confession claim that a Christian shouldn't mention sin anymore. They say that if he mentions sin or failure, it will create a sin consciousness and cause him to sin more. So, the way not to sin is simply by not mentioning sin, and above all, if we fail, we aren't to confess any failure at all.

All of that is strange when we consider that the Apostle Paul mentions sin 17 times in Chapter 6 of Romans alone. Evidently Paul had never heard of this strange doctrine of anti-confession.

We should understand that the Cross of Christ was brought about in the high councils of God, at great price we might quickly add, simply because of sin. No, a believer should not dwell on sin. He should not dwell on the failure because it has now been cleansed and washed, upon our proper confession we might quickly add.

THE AWFULNESS OF SIN

Confession to the Lord of our wrongdoings, at least when wrongdoings are committed, helps us to understand how bad that sin really is. When we confess our sins to the Lord, we are admitting to Him that we are wrong, which is necessary. We are admitting that He is right and that we have wronged Him. In other words, we are saying the same thing about ourselves that God is saying. As stated, this helps us to understand how bad sin is and how wonderful God is.

THE GREAT CONFESSION

All one has to do is read Psalm 51, which is a psalm of David, a prayer of repentance that he prayed regarding his terrible sin with Bath-sheba against her husband Uriah.

This is what he said, which completely refutes this erroneous doctrine of anti-confession: *"Have mercy upon me,*

O God, according to Your lovingkindness: according unto the multitude of Your tender mercies blot out my transgressions." So, here he admits his transgressions.

He then said, "Wash me thoroughly from my iniquity, and cleanse me from my sin." How much plainer could it be?

He then followed by saying, "For I acknowledge my transgressions: and my sin is ever before me." Evidently, this anti-confession message never came to David. He then said, "Against You, You only, have I sinned, and done this evil in Your sight: that You might be justified when You speak, and be clear when You judge."

Now, this is only a portion of Psalm 51. Every believer ought to read the entirety of the psalm and understand that when you read it, you are reading the greatest prayer of repentance that's ever been prayed. To be sure, it is a confession that must be made and that God honors.

THE DENIAL BY SOME

Those who teach the error of anti-confession claim that David's prayer was under the old law and since the Cross, it doesn't count.

Please understand that David was not functioning in the law of Moses whatsoever. In fact, he said, "For you desire not sacrifice; else would I give it: You delight not in burnt offering." He wasn't depending on the law of Moses because there was no help from that source, no help whatsoever.

When David said, *"Purge me with hyssop, and I shall be clean: wash me, and I shall be whiter than snow,"* he was reaching back to the deliverance of the children of Israel from Egyptian bondage. The petition, *"Purge me with hyssop"* expresses a figure of speech. *Purge me with the blood,* which on that night in Egypt was sprinkled on the doorposts with a bunch of hyssop (Ex. 12:13, 22), portrayed David's dependence on the blood of the Lamb — the Christ who was to come.

No, I'll say it again, David was not depending on the law of Moses, for there was no help from that source. By faith, he exercised the blood of Jesus Christ, which had not yet been shed, but which, by faith, was made applicable to David and his situation.

Satan is attacking the doctrine of sin today as never before. If he can eliminate sin from the thinking of people, well then, he can eliminate the solution for sin, which is the Cross of Christ.

The world has almost totally abandoned the idea of sin. Now the alcoholic has a disease, the gambler has a disease, etc. I was hearing the other day that those who engage in child molestation are strongly being thought of as having a disease. No, none of that is a disease. It is sin.

The Evil One doesn't have any problem getting the world to deny sin, but he's making great inroads in the church. Please understand that the denial of sin will in no way absolve its terrible destructive power. The stealing, killing, and destroying will continue right on unabated and will increase.

Let me say it again: Man's problem is sin, and man's solution is the Cross of Christ. There is no other solution!

"Upon life's boundless ocean
"Where mighty billows roll,
"I've fixed my hope in Jesus,
"Blest anchor of my soul;
 "When trials fierce assail me
 "As storms are gathering o're,
 "I rest upon His mercy,
"And trust Him evermore."

"He keeps my soul from evil
"And gives me blessed peace,
"His voice has stilled the waters
"And bid their tumult cease;
"My pilot and deliverer,
"To Him I all confide,
"For always when I need Him
"He's at my side."

"He is my friend and Saviour,
"In Him my anchor's cast,
"He drives away my sorrows
"And shields me from the blast;
"By faith I'm looking upward
"Beyond life's troubled sea,
"There I behold a haven
"Prepared for me."

ELIJAH
THE TISHBITE

CHAPTER

7

JEHOSHAPHAT

CHAPTER SEVEN

JEHOSHAPHAT

FOR NEARLY THREE years Syria had not engaged any type of conflict against Israel. This was because of the two great defeats that Syria had suffered at the hands of Israel and because of Ahab's repentance. However, now, Ahab resorted to his old ways.

Ahab would now face Syria again, which, if he had obeyed the Lord to begin with, this war, no doubt, would never have taken place. It would result in the death of Ahab.

At this time, outwardly, all was prosperous with Ahab. He had an ivory palace, but the secret of the Lord was with Elijah, and he knew the doom that was coming upon all of this glory.

There was also an outward reformation. The prophets of Baal do not appear in this chapter, but on the contrary, 400 professed prophets of Jehovah do.

I Kings 22:2 says that Jehoshaphat was asked to join and even sanction the religious effort, and the Bible says that he *"came down to the king of Israel."* He did not only go down topographically but spiritually as well. It was the beginning of an alliance that caused Jehoshaphat and the kings who followed him many problems. How so much better if Ahab had gone *"up"* to Jerusalem, admitted his sin, sacrificed at the great altar before the temple, and pleaded with God to have mercy upon his soul. That is the only alliance God will honor. This alliance in which Jehoshaphat participated was condemned by God from the beginning.

JEHOSHAPHAT WAS THE FOURTH KING OF JUDAH

Jehoshaphat was the first king of Judah to enter into a treaty with the northern kingdom of Israel. He also took one of Ahab's daughters, Athaliah, to marry his son Jehoram (II Chron. 18:1; II Ki. 8:18). None of this was pleasing to the Lord and would cause future problems for Judah. In fact, this association with apostate Israel almost proved Judah's undoing after Jehoshaphat's death (II Ki. 11:1-3).

Yet, in most other ways, Jehoshaphat tried to adhere to the Word of the Lord. He eradicated, which we will see, much of the pagan worship in Judah and provided preachers and teachers of the Mosaic law (II Chron. 17:7-9). He reorganized the legal system by appointing judges in key cities, with an appeals court in Jerusalem (II Chron. 19:4-11).

RAMOTH-GILEAD

This city, turned into a fortress by Syria, actually belonged to the tribe of Manasseh. It was at the very eastern edge of the boundary. It was one of the cities which Ben-hadad had promised to restore when he was defeated by Israel some three years earlier (I Ki. 20:34). Evidently, he had not kept his word. Though such a long time had elapsed, it was still in his hands. So Ahab, now with the help of Jehoshaphat, proposed to take it by force, which should have been freely given some three years earlier. He evidently felt that he could not perform alone, so he sought the help of Jehoshaphat, who, evidently, at this time, had a powerful army. Regrettably, Jehoshaphat foolishly accepted the invitation to join the northern kingdom against Syria. No doubt, there were many reasons he did this, all seeming plausible at the time. However, it was not the will of God at all for him to make this alliance with Ahab, and as with all such alliances, no good would come out of this union, at least no good for Judah.

THE WORLD AND BELIEVERS

The Bible is strong in its teaching of separation from the world but does not teach isolation. We must never forget that while we are *in* the world, we are not *of* the world. The world's system is controlled by Satan, who is our enemy. We are to make no alliances with the world.

Spiritually speaking, the modern church is laying the foundation for its own destruction by using the ways of the world in what is referred to as *"church growth."* In fact, in no place at all does the Bible teach church growth, but rather growth for the believer.

The Scripture says: *"You therefore, beloved, seeing you know these things before* (the Holy Spirit, through Peter, tells those to whom the apostle was writing that they were not without understanding regarding what was being taught), *beware lest you also, being led away with the error of the wicked* (refers to being led away from the Cross), *fall from your own steadfastness* (refers here to the proper application of one's faith; the Cross of Christ must always be the object of the saint's faith; if we shift our faith to anything else, we 'fall' [Gal. 5:4]).

THE CHURCH IS MEANT TO TELL THE WORLD HOW TO LIVE, NOT THE WORLD TELL THE CHURCH HOW TO LIVE ...

"But grow in grace (presents the only way the saint can grow), *and in the knowledge of our Lord and Saviour Jesus Christ.* (This 'knowledge' refers not only to who Christ is [the Lord of glory], but, as well, what He did in order that we might be redeemed, which points to the Cross.) *To Him be glory both now and forever. Amen* (This refers to such belonging to Him because He is the one who paid the price for man's redemption.)" (II Pet. 3:17-18).

Not only is the modern church employing the ways of the world to fill its pews, but, as well, it has by and large ceased to preach the gospel, but rather a message of its own devisings. The great Bible doctrines, such as sin, the Holy Spirit, sanctification, grace, justification, heaven, hell, etc., are all but presently ignored, with the message now being that of morality and motivation. However, the morality being preached is by and large a *"be good"* and *"do good"* morality. It does not address at all the bondages and powers of darkness that are controlled by Satan, which steal, kill, and virtually destroy the so-called believers.

THE POWERS OF DARKNESS

The believer must understand that the great redemption plan of our Lord, which is given to us in His Word, is the only thing that will take down the powers of darkness. It is not to be added to, deleted from, or changed in any manner. Regrettably, it has been and is being changed altogether.

Believers are facing the powers of darkness, and I speak of powers far beyond our comprehension. In other words, there is no way that the believer can overcome these goliaths by any method other than the Cross of Christ and our faith in that finished work. This is what gives us the help of the Holy Spirit, who alone can overcome the powers of darkness.

Now, this is so important that we must say it again. The believer, and I speak of the true believer — the individual who has truly been born again — is not facing in this Christian journey the keeping of minor rules and regulations. He is facing the concentrated powers of darkness, which are so much stronger and so far beyond our own capacity that it defies description. That's the reason we must, without fail, address this thing God's way. Otherwise, we will be ground under.

PAUL

Paul said, *"Finally, my brethren, be strong in the Lord* (be continually strengthened, which one does by constant faith in the Cross), *and in the power of His might.* (This power is at our disposal. The source is Christ, while the means is the Cross, and the way is the Holy Spirit [I Cor. 1:18].)

"Put on the whole armour of God (not just some, but all), *that you may be able to stand against the wiles of the Devil.* (This refers to the 'stratagems' of Satan.)

"For we wrestle not against flesh and blood (our foes are not human; however, Satan constantly uses human beings to carry out his dirty work), *but against principalities* (rulers or beings of the highest rank and order in Satan's kingdom), *against powers* (the rank immediately below the 'principalities'), *against the rulers of the darkness of this world* (those who carry out the instructions of the 'powers'), *against spiritual wickedness in high places.* (This refers to demon spirits.)" (Eph. 6:10-12).

I would hope the reader would understand from reading this, which the Holy Spirit gave to us through Paul, that we are facing formidable foes.

HUMANISTIC PSYCHOLOGY

Regrettably and sadly, the modern church is attempting to face these things with humanistic psychology, which is a joke at best and blasphemy at worst. However, having forsaken the Holy Spirit and, thereby, forsaking the Holy Spirit, which means that the Cross has been abandoned, the modern church has no other recourse except humanistic psychology. It's sad!

The following tells us the spiritual armor we should wear. Quite possibly our explanation will be totally different than anything you, the reader, have ever heard. Unfortunately, when explaining the whole armor of God, most preachers explain the military garb of the Roman soldier. What good does that do anyone?

Paul used those examples because that was the order of the day. However, what they actually represent and mean is that which we should know and understand. Regrettably, the modern church little understands the weapons of our warfare.

WARFARE

To conserve space, I will not go into great detail but will rather simply give the notes from The Expositor's Study Bible. I personally feel that this will amply explain it.

Paul said, *"Wherefore take unto you the whole armour of God* (because of what we face), *that you may be able to withstand in the evil day* (refers to resisting and opposing the powers of darkness), *and having done all, to stand.* (This refers to the believer not giving ground, not a single inch.)

"*Stand therefore, having your loins gird about with truth* (the truth of the Cross), *and having on the breastplate of righteousness* (the righteousness of Christ, which comes strictly by and through the Cross);

"*And your feet shod with the preparation of the gospel of peace* (peace comes through the Cross as well);

"*Above all, taking the shield of faith* (ever making the Cross the object of your faith, which is the only faith God will recognize, and the only faith Satan will recognize), *wherewith you shall be able to quench all the fiery darts of the wicked.* (This represents temptations with which Satan assails the saints.)

"*And take the helmet of salvation* (has to do with the renewing of the mind, which is done by understanding that everything we receive from the Lord comes to us through the Cross), *and the sword of the Spirit, which is the Word of God* (the Word of God is the story of Christ and the Cross)" (Eph. 6:13-17).

THE CROSS OF CHRIST

I hope the reader can see that everything Paul proposed, as it regards the weapons of our warfare, is all centered in and upon the Cross of Christ. That is, when we trace back that which he said to its origination, it always, and without fail, originates with the Cross.

To make it brief, the following can be said: If the believer will place his faith exclusively in Christ and the Cross and not allow it to be moved to something else, the Holy Spirit will then work mightily within our lives because now that our faith is in the truth, we have the righteousness of Christ. In other words, every weapon that is mentioned here has its roots in the Cross. If the believer doesn't understand the Cross as it refers to our sanctification, there is no way that the believer can properly take unto himself *"the whole armour of God."* It simply cannot be done outside of the Cross.

THE DEFEAT OF SATAN

The Cross is where Satan and all of his henchmen were defeated. It was there where all sin was atoned for. It was there where the Lord Jesus Christ totally and completely triumphed over the powers of darkness and of evil. Chapter 6 of Romans and Chapter 2 of Colossians tell us that the Cross of Christ is the answer to the problem, whatever the problem might be, and, in fact, it is the only answer.

(Please see our study guide from the Cross of Christ series, *God's Prescribed Order of Victory, Romans, Chapter 6.*)

Jehoshaphat was flirting with the world, even as so many modern Christians flirt with the world. The end result will never be pleasant. In fact, the losses will be great. The Cross of Christ and the Cross of Christ alone is the answer to the world. This refers to our faith in that finished work. Only there can we abide in Christ and Christ abide in us (Jn. 14:20).

PROPHETS

Remembering how Ahab's late victories had been fore-told by a prophet and had been won by the help of Jehovah, Jehoshaphat might have well supposed that his new ally would be eager to know the Word of the Lord.

The 400 prophets called out by Ahab claimed to be of the Lord but were not. They characterize the myriad of those who call themselves prophets in Christendom today. In fact, there were precious few true prophets of God then, and there are precious few true prophets of God now.

We will see that the falsity of these prophets was evident to Jehoshaphat. The tragedy is that presently the church hardly knows the difference in the prophets who prophesy out of their own minds and those who speak *"thus saith the Lord."*

Elijah was also alive at this time and had already given several messages to Ahab but was now ignored, or perhaps he was elsewhere in the kingdom.

FALSE PROPHETS

What is a false prophet? Actually, the definition is simple to come by.

False prophets are those who call themselves prophets and really have never been called of God, or else, they originally were called of God but have long since compromised that call-ing. As Israel was full of such in the days of Ahab, regrettably and sadly, the modern church is full of the same presently.

A false prophet is the man or woman who says what he thinks the people want to hear instead of *"thus saith the LORD."*

It is amazing in that presently there are all types of prophecies given with dates and names, claiming that something is going to happen at that particular time, and then the date passes and nothing happens. Let it be understood, they who do such things are false. That simply means they aren't of God, I don't care what the advertisement says. A true prophet is first of all a *"preacher of righteousness"* (II Pet. 2:5).

PETER

Concerning false prophets, Simon Peter said: *"But there were false prophets also among the people* (refers to the false prophets who plagued Israel of old), *even as there shall be false teachers among you* (the false teacher is one who presents a way of salvation or a way of sanctification other than the Cross), *who privily shall bring in damnable heresies* (the idea is that these false teachers would teach some true doctrine and then cleverly include false teaching with it; it is the introduction of false teaching alongside the true that makes it very subtle, and which abrogates the true), *even denying the Lord who bought them* (refers to denying the Cross), *and bring upon themselves swift destruction* (upon themselves and upon those who follow them, which refers to the ultimate loss of the soul).

"And many shall follow their pernicious ways (actually most!); *by reason of whom the way of truth shall be evil spo-*

ken of (proclaims the fact that not only is the truth castigated, but the bearer of truth as well! in short, it is a denigration of the Cross).

FEIGNED WORDS

"*And through covetousness shall they with feigned words make merchandise of you* (the people are exploited instead of developed; the underlying cause is 'money'): *whose judgment now of a long time lingers not, and their damnation slumbers not* (the judgment seems to be delayed, but it definitely is not idle; sooner or later all who travel the path of 'damnable heresies,' which refers to any way other than the Cross, will ultimately face 'utter ruin and destruction')" (II Pet. 2:1-3).

True prophets of the Lord are seldom very much appreciated simply because most of the time their message is negative, that which the people do not delight in hearing. Paul had something to say about this as well.

SOUND DOCTRINE

"*For the time will come when they will not endure sound doctrine* ('sound doctrine' pertains to overriding principles: the salvation of the sinner and the sanctification of the saint; the Cross is the answer for both, and is the only answer for both); *but after their own lusts shall they heap to themselves teachers, having itching ears* (refers to the people who have ears that 'itch' for the smooth and comfortable word, and are willing to reward handsomely the man who is sufficiently compromising to speak it; hearers of this type have rejected the truth and prefer to hear the lie);

"And they shall turn away their ears from the truth (those who follow false teachers not only turn away their ears from the truth, but see to it that the ears are always in a position such that they will never come in contact with the truth), *and shall be turned unto fables.* (If it's not the 'Message of the Cross,' then it is 'fables')" (II Tim. 4:3-4).

Prophets were the de facto spiritual leaders of Israel under the old covenant. Apostles fill that role presently, while the office of the prophet continues as always, but with the exception of leadership (Eph. 4:11).

The ratio of the Israel of Ahab's day, as it regarded true and false prophets, was then about 400-to-1. It probably hasn't changed from then until now.

PROSPERITY AND SUCCESS

If it is to be noticed, the message given to Ahab by the false prophets was a message of prosperity and success. The truth, as we shall see, would turn out to be the very opposite. Think about it for a moment: What is the major message today of most charismatic preachers? The answer is simple; it is prosperity and success.

To be sure, everyone wants prosperity and success. In fact, if followed according to His Word, the Lord will always, to a measure, give prosperity and success. Actually, the only true blessings in the world are those which come from the Lord, and they spell prosperity and success, grandly so.

MICAIAH

"And Jehoshaphat said, Is there not here a prophet of the LORD besides, that we might inquire of him?

"And the king of Israel said unto Jehoshaphat, There is yet one man, Micaiah the son of Imlah" (I Ki. 22:7-8).

However, when that is the only message, then something is wrong. Whenever the sins of the people are never called to account and whenever false doctrine is never addressed, you can be sure that whatever type of message is being proclaimed, it's not of the Lord but simply out of the mind of the individual. Once again, the false way characterizes so much of the modern ministry. As it did then, so it does now!

God give us men such as Micaiah that money cannot buy, who will not compromise their message, who will hear only *"thus saith the LORD,"* and who will not be fearful of delivering that Word to a lost and dying world.

No doubt, Micaiah's mocking tone showed that his words were ironic, but Ahab's hollow tone had already proven to Micaiah that he was insincere, that he did not care to know the will of the Lord, and that he wanted prophets who would speak to him smooth things and prophesy deceits (Isa. 30:10).

AHAB

Ahab's feigned desire to hear truth was spoken for the benefit of Jehoshaphat. In reality, he had no desire to hear the truth. Ahab was a false shepherd and whether he believed it or not, he was about to die. It is clear that Ahab had understood perfectly the purport of Micaiah's words.

Micaiah was given a vision of the throne of God and its happenings there, which he now related to both Ahab and Jehoshaphat. The meaning is that Ahab's death in battle had been decreed in the counsels of God, and that the divine wisdom had devised means for accomplishing God's purpose.

As we shall see, we learn from this account, as well as from Job, Chapter 1, that spirits of darkness, as well as Satan, at times, have access to the throne of God. During the coming great tribulation, Satan and all spirits of darkness will be cast out of heaven and allowed no more access (Rev. 12:7-9).

EVIL SPIRITS

This *"lying spirit"* would inspire these false prophets to prophesy the evil that was desired. All of this reveals that God and His heavenly host, including demons on certain occasions, have conferences concerning the affairs of men on earth.

The idea is that God permitted such deception in order to take the place of the rejected truth. If men will not have the truth, they will automatically have a substitute that will be more in harmony with their wicked ways for the time being.

Ahab would not have the truth and would not listen to Jehovah, despite all of the attempts made by the Lord to reach this man. Instead, he would believe lies and listen to his false prophets.

This passage gives an insight into the spirit realm, showing that behind all human acts, there are good and bad spirits seeking to carry out the respective wills of their masters. The Lord protects as long as He can, and when there is nothing else He can do, at least by righteous means, to turn men from their wicked ways, error, and harm, He then permits demon spirits to deceive. This causes the individual in question to go further astray, and in the case of Ahab, even unto death.

MICAIAH AND ZEDEKIAH

The prophecy of Zedekiah and the prophecy of Micaiah, as is obvious, were totally different. The first spoke of blessing, while the latter spoke of doom. Both could not be right. In essence, it is the same presently.

Thousands of false prophets are prophesying blessings and victory upon an apostate church, while the few true prophets are attempting to call the church to repentance. As with Ahab, both cannot be right.

Ahab was killed, which was predicted by Micaiah, and concerning Zedekiah hiding himself, it happened exactly as stated.

The bravery of Micaiah condemns the cowardice of Jehoshaphat. Jehoshaphat should have stepped down from his throne, thrown his mantle around the courageous prophet, and valiantly taken his stand at his side. Regrettably, he didn't!

There is no one more cowardly and contemptible than a Christian who walks with the religious world. Micaiah was led away to prison and to torture, and Jehoshaphat raised neither a hand nor a voice on his behalf. One's heart is grieved at the prospect!

THE TRUE PROPHET

Micaiah was his name. His name means *"who is like Jehovah."*

No doubt, while the false prophets were treated royally by Ahab, Micaiah was brought from prison. Such it was then, and spiritually speaking, such it is now.

When Micaiah was retrieved by the messenger, the advice to him was that he speak good words to the king. The prophet's answer was straight and to the point, *"What the* LORD *says unto me, that will I speak"* (I Ki. 22:14).

Ahab probably spoke to Micaiah with sarcasm, and the prophet answered him in the same manner. However, the way in which he answered told the king, and, in fact, all who were there, that what he was saying was not what the Lord had given unto him. So, Ahab demanded of him that the truth be told.

To be sure, his message was scathing! He saw Israel totally defeated and, as well, Ahab killed.

Then Micaiah gave us a glimpse into the spirit world that is totally unlike anything else given in the Bible.

THE VISION

Micaiah claimed that he *"saw the LORD sitting on His throne, and all the host of heaven standing by Him on His right hand and on His left"* (I Ki. 22:19).

John the Revelator also had a vision of the throne of God; however, it was far different than that had by the Prophet Micaiah.

At any rate, we learn from this vision and other accounts in the Word of God that matters on earth are first of all decided in heaven. Some have the erroneous idea that Satan runs the show. He doesn't! He does what the Lord of glory tells him he can do — no more, no less!

He heard the Lord asking the question, *"Who shall persuade Ahab, that he may go up and fall at Ramoth-gilead?"* (I Ki. 22:20).

Consequently, we are able to observe the conference that was held in heaven as it regarded the fate of this king of Israel. It is revealing to say the least!

THE LYING SPIRIT

At a point in time, the Scripture says, as it regards this conference and what to do with Ahab, *"And there came forth a spirit, and stood before the LORD, and said, I will persuade him"* (I Ki. 22:21).

It may come as a surprise to many Christians that Satan still has access to heaven, according to the account given to us in Job, Chapters 1 and 2. As well, we also see from this text that there are evil spirits present there.

As to exactly what they are allowed to do, we aren't told. This is a demon spirit that is addressed here. So, if there is one evil spirit in heaven, no doubt, there are many others.

The Scripture tells us that one day soon, actually, at about the midpoint of the coming great tribulation, Satan and all of his evil hosts will be cast out of heaven, having no more access there.

The account says: *"And there was war in heaven* (pertains to the 'mystery of God' being finished)*: Michael and his angels fought against the dragon; and the dragon fought and his angels* (this pertains to Satan and all the angels who followed him being cast out of heaven, which will take place, as stated, at about the midpoint of the great tribulation; why the Lord has allowed Satan and his minions to remain in heaven all of this time, we aren't told; it is a 'mystery,' but it will now be finished),

"And prevailed not (Satan will then be defeated; incidentally, it is not Satan who instigates this war, but rather the archangel Michael at the command of God); *neither was their place found any more in heaven* (joins with the close of the book of Revelation, where the Evil One has no more place on earth, as well, but rather the place of torment forever and forever [Rev. 20:10]).

THE GREAT DRAGON

"And the great dragon was cast out, that old serpent, called the Devil, and Satan (he is referred to as 'the great

dragon' because of his propensity to 'steal, kill, and destroy' [Jn. 10:10]; he is the 'old serpent' because in his first appearance in the Bible, he chose to work through a serpent; thereby, he is what the curse caused the serpent to be, wryly subtle and treacherous), *which deceives the whole world* (deception is his greatest weapon; he deceives and is himself deceived): *he was cast out into the earth, and his angels were cast out with him* (pronounces the beginning of the end for this evil monster)" (Rev. 12:7-9).

The evil spirit spoke to the Lord concerning Ahab and said, *"I will go forth, and I will be a lying spirit in the mouth of all his prophets."* The Lord then said to him, *"You shall persuade him, and prevail also: go forth, and do so"* (I Ki. 22:22).

Micaiah then said, *"Behold, the LORD has put a lying spirit in the mouth of all these your prophets, and the LORD has spoken evil concerning you"* (I Ki. 22:23).

EVIL SPIRITS

All of this tells us that evil spirits are far more predominant than most realize. We are here told that all false prophets are more or less controlled by demon spirits.

Paul said: *"Now the Spirit* (Holy Spirit) *speaks expressly* (pointedly), *that in the latter times* (the times in which we now live, the last of the last days, which begin the fulfillment of end-time prophecies) *some shall depart from the faith* (anytime Paul uses the term 'the faith,' in short, he is referring to the Cross; so, we are told here that some will depart from the Cross as the means of salvation and victory), *giving heed to seducing spirits* (evil spirits, i.e., 'religious spirits,' making something seem like what it isn't), *and doctrines of devils* (should have been translated, 'doctrines of demons'; the 'seducing spirits' entice believers away from the true faith, causing them to believe 'doctrines inspired by demon spirits');

"*Speaking lies in hypocrisy* (concerns the teachers of these 'doctrines of demons,' which pertain to anything that leads one away from the Cross)" (I Tim. 4:1-2).

Actually, the whole world of religion is infested with demon spirits.

As we have stated elsewhere in this volume, religion is that which is devised by men, which purports to draw one closer to God or to better oneself in some way. Inasmuch as it is devised by men, this means that it is unacceptable to God and, consequently, is controlled more or less by demon spirits.

DECEPTION

From the account given to us here of this lying spirit who filled the mouths of these false prophets, we learn that those who listen to such become like what they hear. In other words, the deceiving spirit takes them over, and they become deceived. In fact, untold millions have lost their souls in that fashion.

This means that every believer must be very, very careful as to the preacher they follow and the church they attend. Nothing is more important!

Let us say it another way: If the preacher is not preaching the Cross, this means that he is not preaching the gospel. There certainly are some preachers who are godly, and yet, do not understand the Cross; thereby, they preach all the light they have, and God blesses it. However, to be sure, that type of man or woman will ultimately be led to the complete truth.

The facts are, most preachers do not know anything about the Cross of Christ, especially as it regards our sanctification, and, in fact, they have no desire to know anything about the Cross. They are immersed in the world of religion and as such, are more or less guided by demon spirits.

This is so important that we must say it again: All deception comes from evil spirits. If a believer listens to a preacher who is himself deceived, the listener will be likewise affected. Tragically, this means that churches are probably sending more people to hell than all the liquor joints in the world.

JEHOSHAPHAT AND MICAIAH

It is sad to read that after this prophecy was given by Micaiah to Ahab, Jehoshaphat watched Ahab put Micaiah back in prison, no doubt, to be tortured, and never lifted a voice on his behalf. As well, he heard this man of God state, *"I saw all Israel scattered upon the hills, as sheep that have not a shepherd: and the LORD said, These have no master"* (I Ki. 22:17), meaning that Ahab would be killed along with Israel being defeated.

This should have been enough to warn Jehoshaphat not to have part in this battle. In fact, he would have been killed had it not been for the intervention of the Lord.

Why did Jehoshaphat do what he did?

Didn't this man know the wickedness of Ahab? Did he not believe the Prophet Micaiah, especially considering the detailed account he gave of the instructions of the Lord concerning Ahab?

HEARKEN!

All of this shows us that it's possible for even the godly to be led astray. If we associate ourselves with the wicked, their deception sooner or later will become our deception. The true church must have no truck whatsoever with the apostate church. There can be no middle ground, no compromise, and no association. While we must pray for them and love them, still, the line is drawn, and we must not cross that line.

As Micaiah was being led away, his last words were, *"Hearken, O people, every one of you"* (I Ki. 22:28).

No doubt, many were in that audience that day, and all heard what he had to say. There is little evidence that any of them did what the Spirit said to do: *"Hearken!"*

Is the Holy Spirit through His true prophets saying the same thing today to the modern church: *"Hearken, O people, every one of you?"*

TWO ROYAL FOOLS

"So the king of Israel and Jehoshaphat the king of Judah went up to Ramoth-gilead" (I Ki. 22:29).

Two royal fools at once meet in these verses. Jehoshaphat was a fool to go into battle in his royal robes — at Ahab's suggestion I might add — or to go at all for that matter. Ahab was a greater fool to propose to escape the divine doom pronounced upon him by going into battle without his royal robes.

The Syrians intended to kill Ahab! So much for the covenant that Ben-hadad had made with Ahab (I Ki. 20:34).

Ahab's attempt to disguise himself served no purpose. A Syrian archer shot, not even knowing where he was shooting, and the Lord had the arrow and Ahab to meet in the same place. It should be understood that one cannot outwit the Lord. The Lord had stated that Ahab would die in this battle, so irrespective as to what he did, his death was a foregone conclusion.

The record is replete, I think, with the fact that the Lord loved Ahab and sought to save him again and again, but all to no avail.

"So Ahab slept with his fathers; and Ahaziah his son reigned in his stead" (I Ki. 22:40).

The name *Ahaziah* means *"whom Jehovah upholds."* Ahab giving his son this name suggests that notwithstanding his idolatries, Ahab had knowledge of the Lord. However, despite the constant spiritual tug, he wouldn't serve the Lord.

THE WORD OF THE LORD

As it regards Ahab, there was very little that could be done with such a stubborn man — one consecrated to demon worship and demon prophets. The godly Prophet Micaiah had been sent to Ahab, but Ahab would not receive Jehovah's instructions. In this case, II Thessalonians 2:8-12 is clearly illustrated. Because he and his associates had no love for the truth that they might be saved, God sent them *"strong delusion, that they should believe a lie: that they all might be damned who believed not the truth, but had pleasure in unrighteousness."*

The idea is that God permitted such deception to take the place of the rejected truth. If men will not have the truth, they will automatically have a substitute that will be more in harmony with their wicked ways for the time being.

Ahab would not have the truth and would not listen to Jehovah, but he would have lies and listen to his false prophets, which brought about his death.

The account of all of this gives us an insight into the spirit realm, showing that behind all human acts, there are good and bad spirits seeking to carry out the respected wills of their masters. The Lord protects as long as He can. When there is nothing else He can do to turn men from their wicked ways, error, and harm, He then permits demon spirits to deceive and cause them to go further astray, in this case, even unto death.

A SECRET ROOT OF SPIRITUAL WEAKNESS

Verse 29 says, *"So the king of Israel and Jehoshaphat the king of Judah went up to Ramoth-gilead."*

This alliance with Ahab revealed a secret root of spiritual weakness in Jehoshaphat's heart, the fruit of which was disastrous to his children. Jehoshaphat did not help Ahab to return to truth, but Ahab helped Jehoshaphat to be unfaithful to Jehovah.

It is amazing as to how that men will hear the Word of the Lord and know beyond the shadow of a doubt that it is the Word of the Lord but still will not heed that which is stated, or else, will register unbelief. This was the case, at least as it regarded this battle with the Syrians and as it regarded both Ahab and Jehoshaphat.

When the Prophet Micaiah gave his word from the Lord, even going into detail as to what would happen, it would seem that Ahab would have fallen on his face and repented. He was not without knowledge regarding the prophets of the Lord. However, Ahab, as is obvious, chose to believe his false prophets and then locked up Micaiah so he could not say anything else, at least that could be heard.

Ahab had had many opportunities to repent and many instances where he had seen, witnessed, and observed some of the greatest miracles ever performed by the Lord, but all to no avail.

REBELLION

Let the following be understood: With each instance of rebellion toward God, irrespective as to whom it might be, the heart grows harder, meaning that it becomes more difficult to believe the truth, even though it's obvious before one's very own eyes. This was the case with Ahab, and it has been and is the case with untold millions.

Concerning rebellion, the Scripture says, *"For rebellion is as the sin of witchcraft, and stubbornness is as iniquity and idolatry"* (I Sam. 15:23).

Please notice how the Holy Spirit presents the various words. How is *"rebellion as the sin of witchcraft?"*

If one rebels against God's way, which is rebellion against His Word, then such an individual sets about to devise his own means and way. This means that he tries to manipulate the spirit world, whether he understands such or not, and that is witchcraft.

THE CROSS

The believer can reach God only through Jesus Christ and can reach Jesus Christ only through the Cross.

Please note the following:

- The only way to God is through Jesus Christ (Jn. 14:6).
- The only way to Jesus Christ is through the Cross (Lk. 9:23).
- The only way to the Cross is a denial of self (Lk. 9:23).

If we attempt to function in any other manner, and I'm speaking of a manner outside of the Cross, then we are devising our own ways, thereby, rebelling against God and engaging in witchcraft.

Stubbornness is linked with rebellion, which speaks of an intractable spirit, a spirit that demands its own way, and that is the problem with mankind. We want our way instead of God's ways. Such is sin, i.e., iniquity, and is a form of idolatry.

Let's put it this way: anything other than faith in Christ and what He has done for us at the Cross is, in one way or the other, idolatry.

The more that an individual yields to the Lord, the easier that it is to yield, and conversely, the more that one rebels against the Lord, sadly and regrettably, the easier it becomes to rebel.

Let's put it another way: If one wants righteousness, the Lord will see to it that one obtains righteousness. Conversely, if one wants unrighteousness, the Lord will see to it that one has unrighteousness.

JEHOSHAPHAT

In this chapter, Jehoshaphat's reign is disposed of in 10 verses, but 102 verses are devoted to it in II Chronicles.

The meaning is this: To the unspiritual eye, Jehoshaphat would have been uninteresting beside the glitter of Ahab. However, to the spiritual eye, which is given in II Chronicles, Ahab is of no interest at all, with Jehoshaphat demanding God's attention. Both books of Kings portray events as men saw them, with both books of the Chronicles portraying events as God saw them.

"And he walked in all the ways of Asa his father; he turned not aside from it, doing that which was right in the eyes of the Lord: *nevertheless the high places were not taken away; for the people offered and burnt incense yet in the high places"* (I Ki. 22:43).

As it concerns the people of Verse 43 continuing to burn incense in the high places, there was to be only one place of sacrifice, and that was to be at the temple in Jerusalem. So, it seems that the Holy Spirit was displeased with Jehoshaphat's actions in not taking away the high places.

For some 70 years, from the date of their separation to the time of Asa's death, there had been little peace between Judah and Israel. Jehoshaphat sought to remedy this situation but, at times, as we have seen, by using methods that were displeasing to the Lord.

THE SODOMITES

"And the remnant of the sodomites, which remained in the days of his father Asa, he took out of the land" (I Ki. 22:46).

There seems to have been only a few sodomites left; however, the Holy Spirit is quick to proclaim the fact that Jehoshaphat removed even these few. Too often the child of God is willing to allow *"the remnant"* of evil to remain. The Holy Spirit demands that everything that is evil be taken out, which can only be done by the believer placing his faith exclusively in Christ and the Cross. This then gives the Holy Spirit latitude to work within our lives, thereby, bringing about the desired victory (Rom. 6:1-14; 8:1-11; Col. 2:10-15).

As we shall see, Jehoshaphat formed an alliance with Ahab's son, Ahaziah; however, the Lord was not pleased with this alliance and, thereby, destroyed the ships. Jehoshaphat would not permit Ahaziah to join him after that. In other words, Jehoshaphat seems to have finally gotten the message.

JEHOSHAPHAT

There were some lapses in the life and living of Jehoshaphat, king of Judah; however, despite those lapses, the Holy Spirit states of him, *"He turned not aside from it, doing that which was right in the eyes of the LORD."*

However, then the Holy Spirit adds, *"Nevertheless the high places were not taken away; for the people offered and burnt incense yet in the high places"* (I Ki. 22:43).

The idea of these statements is, despite the wrong directions that Jehoshaphat sometimes took, still, his heart was toward God. This means that he desired to please the Lord and evidently was quick to repent whenever he did wrong.

Let it be understood that there is no human being who has ever lived but that the word *nevertheless* is placed by their name. This includes even the godliest among us, whomever that may be or may have been. In other words, there has only been one perfect man, and that Man was and is the Lord Jesus Christ. *Nevertheless* has to be added to all others.

AN OLD SIN IS AN EASY SIN

"Then said Ahaziah the son of Ahab unto Jehoshaphat, Let my servants go with your servants in the ships. But Jehoshaphat would not" (I Ki. 22:49).

And yet, II Chronicles 20:37 proclaims that the ships were broken, according to a prophecy of Eliezer, the son of Dodavah, because Jehoshaphat had, in fact, joined himself with Ahaziah.

It seems that the fleet had actually been built by the two kings who had joined together in this effort. After the ships were broken (we do not know how that happened but, no doubt, had been brought about by the Lord), Ahaziah proposed either to repair the damaged vessels or to construct a second fleet. This proposal was declined by Jehoshaphat, evidently taking the warning given by the Prophet Eliezer.

The Lord had not been pleased with Jehoshaphat joining alliance with Ahab, and now He was no more pleased with him joining alliance with Ahab's wicked son, Ahaziah. As stated, an old sin is an easy sin.

THE KINGS OF JUDAH

Elijah, in fact, was sent to the northern kingdom of Israel and not the southern kingdom of Judah. For quite a period of time here, he doesn't seem to have been involved in either kingdom but would come once again on the scene shortly. There is no explanation given as to why at this time there was no movement on his part as it regarded the northern kingdom of Israel and Ahab. Still, what was done, I'm sure it's what the Holy Spirit wanted. Actually, there was a time frame of approximately three years in which we heard nothing from Elijah, but then suddenly, as we shall soon see, he appeared on the scene once again.

The kings of Judah were very important to the work of God and, in fact, to the entirety of the world. It was because they were in the lineage of David, from which would come Christ the Redeemer (II Sam. 7:16).

Verse 53 of Chapter 22 of I Kings proclaims at least one of the reasons, and, in fact, the primary reason, that the Lord was sorely displeased with Jehoshaphat forming an alliance with Ahaziah. The wickedness of the northern kingdom would ever grow deeper until the Lord finally allowed them to be taken over by Assyria and led into captivity.

SIN

As we see from the ways of Israel and its wicked kings to whom Elijah had been sent, the problem of sin ever grew worse. The Scripture says that Ahaziah, Ahab's son, *"did evil in the sight of the LORD"* (I Ki. 22:52). The Holy Spirit delineates three particulars:

1. He walked in the way of his father Ahab.

2. He walked in the way of his mother Jezebel, *"For he served Baal, and worshipped him, and provoked to anger the* LORD *God of Israel, according to all that his father had done"* (I Ki. 22:53).

3. He also walked *"in the way of Jeroboam the son of Nebat, who made Israel to sin"* (I Ki. 22:52). This pertained to calf worship.

Sin ever gets worse and worse. It cannot be ameliorated, slowed, brought to heel, or in any way stopped by the stratagems or efforts of men, irrespective of what these efforts might be.

Let us say it again: There is no way in the natural or by the stratagems of man that sin can be stopped. Despite all of man's efforts, it continues to get worse and worse until all is destroyed.

THE ONLY ANSWER FOR SIN IS THE CROSS OF CHRIST

Whatever the problem is, one can be certain that it is sin in some way.

There is an answer for sin, but only one answer, and that is the Cross of Christ.

The Scripture says: *"But this Man* (this Priest, Christ Jesus), *after He had offered one sacrifice for sins forever* (speaks of the Cross), *sat down on the right hand of God* (refers to the great contrast with the priests under the Levitical system, who never sat down because their work was never completed; the work of Christ was a 'finished work' and needed no repetition);

"From henceforth expecting till His enemies be made His footstool. (These enemies are Satan and all the fallen angels and demon spirits, plus all who follow Satan.)

"For by one offering He has perfected forever them who are sanctified. (Everything one needs is found in the Cross [Gal. 6:14])" (Heb. 10:12-14).

JOHN THE BAPTIST

John the Baptist said of Christ: *"Behold the Lamb of God* (proclaims Jesus as the sacrifice for sin, in fact, the sin offering, whom all the multiple millions of offered lambs had represented), *which takes away the sin of the world* (animal blood could only cover sin, it could not take it away; but Jesus offering Himself as the perfect sacrifice took away the sin of the world, at least for those who will believe; He not only cleansed acts of sin but, as well, addressed the root cause [Col. 2:10-15])" (Jn. 1:29).

That's the reason it is so very, very important — actually, the single most important thing in the world regarding the salvation of souls — that the Cross of Christ be preached. If the preacher doesn't look at Christ as the source and the Cross as the means through which the Holy Spirit works, then whatever it is that the preacher is proclaiming is not the gospel. That's why Paul said, *"We preach Christ crucified"* (I Cor. 1:23).

"For God so loved this sinful world,
"His Son He freely gave,
"That whosoever would believe,
"Eternal life shall have."

"I was a wayward, wandering child,
"A slave to sin and fear,
"Until this blessed promise fell
"Like music on my ear."

"The 'whosoever' of the Lord,
"I trusted was for me;
"I took Him at His gracious word,
"From sin He set me free."

"Eternal life begun below,
"Now fills my heart and soul;
"I'll sing His praise forevermore,
"Whose blood has made me whole."

ELIJAH
THE TISHBITE

CHAPTER

8

IT IS ELIJAH THE TISHBITE

CHAPTER EIGHT

IT IS ELIJAH THE TISHBITE

EVEN THOUGH ELIJAH was silent for about three years of time at this particular juncture, still, we feel that the information given in I and II Kings, concerning the direction of these two nations, is of extreme importance. So, we elected to include the account.

The material given in II Kings, which is a continuation of I Kings, actually begins about 80 years after the division of the kingdom, with parallel accounts given from both kingdoms.

The northern kingdom, called Israel, lasted about 130 years after the division before falling in 722 B.C. to the Assyrians, whose capital was Nineveh. The southern kingdom, called Judah, was in existence another 136 years before it fell to the Babylonians in 586 B.C. prior to the final fall of Judah. Many of the people were taken captive to Babylon, the capital, in 605 B.C. and 596 B.C., with the latter being the final fall of Judah.

WHY IS THE ACCOUNT OF THESE
TWO KINGDOMS SO IMPORTANT?

First of all, they are immensely important simply because these people were God's people, despite the fact that the majority of them did not really live for God. In fact, there were always two Israels, so to speak, and I'm not speaking of the southern and the northern kingdoms but the entirety of the people of Israel in general. I speak of those who served the Lord, of which the number was always few, and of those who did not serve the Lord, but yet, were Israelites. Actually, it is the same in the modern church.

There are untold professors of religion in the church; however, there are only a few, and only the Lord knows the number, who have actually been born again, and who are actually serving the Lord.

Whatever the Israelites' state or status, spiritually speaking, they were the only people in the world who knew Jehovah. This means they were monotheistic, meaning they worshipped one God and, in fact, were the only people on planet Earth who did so. All the other nations of the world were polytheistic, meaning they worshipped all types of gods, actually demon spirits.

Considering that Israel alone was the light of the world, it should be understood as to why they were so very, very important. That's the reason their fall was so catastrophic; there were none to take their place.

TO GIVE THE WORLD THE WORD OF GOD

There is absolutely nothing in the world more important than the Word of God. It is important simply because it is the Word of God and, thereby, proclaims the way of life and living, and above all, is the blueprint for eternity. It is Israel who gave the Bible to the world. Every part of it, as far as we know, was written by the prophets of old or the apostles of the New Testament. They were all Jewish, with possibly the exception of Luke.

Some claim that Luke was a Gentile. Perhaps he was; however, it is my personal thought that Luke was actually Jewish. Nevertheless, through these men of God, spanning a time frame of approximately 1,600 years, the Bible was ultimately given to the human race.

Moses, the great lawgiver, was the first writer of the Bible, writing the Pentateuch, the first five books of the Bible. It is also believed that Moses may very well have collaborated with Job in writing the book that bears the name of Job. If, in fact, that is the case, the book of Job would be the oldest book on the face of the earth and was probably written while Moses was at the backside of the desert. No doubt, Genesis was written at that time as well.

The canon of Scripture was closed out approximately 1,600 years later by John the Beloved, who wrote the book of Revelation while incarcerated as a prisoner on the island of Patmos.

THE COMING OF THE MESSIAH

As well, and even more important, the Jewish people served, one might say, as the womb of the Messiah. I speak of the Lord Jesus Christ who was born of the Virgin Mary, and who was the Son of the living God. He was God manifest in the flesh (Isa. 7:14). All of this means that Jesus Christ was very God and very man. He wasn't half man and half God, but rather fully God and fully man! While during His incarnation, He never ceased to be God, still, during that time, He laid aside the expression of His deity while never losing possession of His deity.

He came but for one purpose, and that was to go to the Cross. There He would offer Himself as a sacrifice for sin, making it possible for sinful man to be saved and to come into the very presence of God.

THE JEWISH PEOPLE

The Jewish people were raised up for the very purpose of bringing the Son of God into the world. Unfortunately, they did not recognize Him when He came, or if they did, they refused to admit it and demanded that He be crucified as an impostor. For that act, they have suffered untold agony for nearly 2,000 years and have been scattered all over the world. However, in 1948, in fulfillment of Bible prophecy, the nation of Israel was reborn in their ancient homeland. The ultimate conclusion will be their full restoration, which will take place at the second coming. Then, all Jews in the world will accept Christ as their Saviour and their Lord, realizing that the One they crucified was in reality their Messiah. Willingly, gloriously, and gladly they will accept Him, and do so without reservation. This is yet to come, but most assuredly, it shall come! The formation of Israel as a state was and is a harbinger of this coming event. Truly, as it has been stated, Israel is God's prophetic time clock.

In other words, one can look at Israel and pretty much tell the time that the great prophecies of Daniel and others are to be fulfilled. In fact, the world is on the very eve of their fulfillment, even though it really doesn't know or understand such.

THE LEADING NATION IN THE WORLD

When Jesus Christ comes back and sets up His kingdom, which will last for 1,000 years (Rev., Chpt. 20), Israel will then carry out the will of God, even as the Lord originally intended. They will then be the priestly nation of the world, even as Ezekiel proclaims in the last nine chapters of his book.

It's difficult for some to realize that the tiny state of Israel will be the leading nation in the world at that time; however, they will be for many and varied reasons.

First of all, Israel was raised up by the Lord for this very purpose. Admittedly, as stated, they went astray and lost their way. Actually, their rejection of Jesus Christ when the kingdom was offered to them, which was done at His first advent, has subjected the world to 2,000 additional years of trouble and heartache (Mat., Chpt. 24). However, finally, Israel will carry out her role in the world that was originally intended. It cannot be done without Jesus Christ.

THE BLESSING UPON ISRAEL

Anything that God conceives and that to which He gives birth, He blesses, at least as long as His will is followed. He will also bless those who bless His work. Consequently, as it regards Israel, even when they were in the loins of Abraham and the womb of Sarah, the Lord said to Abraham, and I quote from The Expositor's Study Bible:

"And I will make of you a great nation (the nation which God made of Abraham has changed the world and exists even unto this hour; in fact, this nation 'Israel' still has a great part to play, which will take place in the coming kingdom age), *and I will bless you, and make your name great* (according to Scripture, 'to bless' means 'to increase'; the builders of the Tower of Babel sought to 'make us a name,' whereas God took this man, who forsook all, and 'made his name great'); *and you shall be a blessing:* (concerns itself with the greatest blessing of all. It is the glory of Abraham's faith. God would give this man the meaning of salvation, which is 'justification by faith,' which would come about through the Lord Jesus Christ and what Christ would do on the Cross. Concerning this, Jesus said of Abraham, 'Your father Abraham rejoiced to see My day: and he saw it, and was glad' [Jn. 8:56].)

"And I will bless them who bless you (to bless Israel, or any believer for that matter, guarantees the blessings of God), *and curse him who curses you* (to curse Israel or any believer guarantees that one will be cursed by God): *and in you shall all families of the earth be blessed.* (It speaks of Israel, which sprang from the loins of Abraham and the womb of Sarah, giving the world the Word of God and, more particularly, bringing the Messiah into the world. Through Christ, every family in the world who desires blessing from God can have that blessing, i.e., 'justification by faith')" (Gen. 12:2-3).

THE ENTIRETY OF THE WORLD

All of mankind should read these words given by the Lord as it regards blessing Israel, which will then guarantee the blessings of God. Unfortunately, most of the world ignores that which was said by the Lord to Abraham. Despite the fact that these words were uttered some 4,000 years ago, they're just as true now as they were then.

This means that the Palestinians, the Muslims, and all others who oppose Israel cannot win, irrespective of their proposed strength or numbers. God is against them because they are against Israel. Actually, as it regards nations, the United States is about the only friend in the world that Israel has. To be sure, that friendship is based exclusively upon the hundreds of thousands of truly born-again Christians in America who demand that support. Tragically, that number is getting smaller all the time. If, in fact, the United States ever turns its back on Israel, despite our economic and military strength, this will strike the death blow to this nation. The Lord meant and means what He said. He will bless those who bless Israel and, in fact, those who bless any believer, even in this present time. He will curse those who curse Israel and those who attempt to hurt or hinder modern believers.

WHAT DOES IT MEAN TO BE CURSED BY GOD?

Due to the fact of being lawbreakers, every person in this world who is not born again is cursed by God, for the Bible clearly says:

"For as many as are of the works of the law are under the curse: for it is written, Cursed is every one who continues not in all things which are written in the book of the law to do them" (Gal. 3:10).

Whether they realize it or not, this means, as stated, that every person in the world who is not born again is under the curse of God. That means that such a person is in serious peril. In fact, that's the cause of all war, poverty, superstition, bondage, darkness, etc. The only light in this world is that which pertains to believers, who derive such light from the Lord Jesus Christ.

Jesus said, *"You are the salt of the earth ... You are the light of the world"* (Mat. 5:13-14).

However, when a person accepts Jesus Christ as his Saviour and his Lord, at that moment, every single curse is lifted, and it's all because of what Jesus did at the Cross. In other words, the Cross of Christ canceled every curse, and I mean every curse.

Paul said: *"Christ has redeemed us from the curse of the law, being made a curse for us: for it is written, Cursed is every one who hangs on a tree* (Jesus hung upon the Cross, i.e., 'the tree' [Deut. 21:22-23])*"* (Gal. 3:13).

Any preacher, or anyone for that matter, who claims that true believers are still under a curse of some nature, simply does not understand the Word of God, meaning he does not understand the Cross. What Jesus did at the Cross canceled every curse, atoned for every sin, and broke every bondage of darkness and, as well, defeated Satan, his fallen angels, and demon spirits.

SATAN DEFEATED

Paul said, and I quote directly from The Expositor's Study Bible: *"And you are complete in Him* (the satisfaction of every spiritual want is found in Christ, made possible by the Cross), *which is the head of all principality and power* (His headship extends not only over the church, which voluntarily serves Him, but over all forces that are opposed to Him as well [Phil. 2:10-11]):

"In whom also you are circumcised with the circumcision made without hands (that which is brought about by the Cross [Rom. 6:3-5]), *in putting off the body of the sins of the flesh by the circumcision of Christ* (refers to the old carnal nature that is defeated by the believer placing his faith totally in the Cross, which gives the Holy Spirit latitude to work):

"*Buried with Him in baptism* (does not refer to water baptism, but rather to the believer baptized into the death of Christ, which refers to the crucifixion and Christ as our substitute [Rom. 6:3-4]), *wherein also you are risen with Him through the faith of the operation of God, who has raised Him from the dead.* (This does not refer to our future physical resurrection, but to that spiritual resurrection from a sinful state into divine life. We died with Him, we are buried with Him, and we rose with Him [Rom. 6:3-5], and herein lies the secret to all spiritual victory.)

"*And you, being dead in your sins and the uncircumcision of your flesh* (speaks of spiritual death [i.e., 'separation from God'], which sin does!), *has He quickened together with Him* (refers to being made spiritually alive, which is done through being 'born again'), *having forgiven you all trespasses* (the Cross made it possible for all manner of sins to be forgiven and taken away);

"*Blotting out the handwriting of ordinances that was against us* (pertains to the law of Moses, which was God's standard of righteousness that man could not reach), *which was contrary to us* (law is against us simply because we are unable to keep its precepts, no matter how hard we try), *and took it out of the way* (refers to the penalty of the law being removed), *nailing it to His Cross* (the law with its decrees was abolished in Christ's death, as if crucified with Him);

"*And having spoiled principalities and powers* (Satan and all of his henchmen were defeated at the Cross by Christ atoning for all sin; sin was the legal right Satan had to hold man in captivity; with all sin atoned, he has no more legal right to hold anyone in bondage), *He* (Christ) *made a show of them openly* (what Jesus did at the Cross was in the face of the whole universe), *triumphing over them in it.* (The triumph is complete, and it was all done for us, meaning we can walk in power and perpetual victory due to the Cross)" (Col. 2:10-15).

CHRISTIAN PSYCHOLOGY?

Moab had originally been conquered by David (II Sam. 8:2; 23:20) and after the division of Judah and Israel, it passed to Israel. The Moabites were greatly oppressed by Omri and Ahab, and on the death of Ahab, Mesha, king of Moab, rebelled and gained independence.

Ahaziah cast away the last remnant of faith in the salvation afforded by the Lord, which was believed in by the patriarchs of Israel, and consulted a foreign oracle as if the voice of God was silent in his own country. By and large, the sin of the modern church is little different from the sin of Ahaziah. Having opted for the fallacy of humanistic and atheistic psychology, it has, for the most part, forsaken the God of the Bible. It has tried to cover its sin by labeling its foray into modernism with the term, *"Christian psychology."* However, such does not exist. Psychology is not a true science because its various methods of treatment are worthy of a Roman circus. It has its roots in atheism, evolution, and humanism. It is the total opposite of the Bible. So-called Christian psychology is no different whatsoever from any other type of psychology. The name *Christian* is given to it only to deceive a gullible Christian public that has basically forsaken the Bible.

IS ALL TRUTH GOD'S TRUTH?

The action of Ahaziah presents a complete and absolute denial of the divinity of Jehovah. To consult a foreign oracle is equivalent to saying that the voice of God is wholly silent in one's own land. This was going further in apostasy than Ahab had gone.

As stated, the modern church is doing the same thing in its acceptance of humanistic psychology. It does so under the farce and of the guise that all truth is God's truth. The meaning is: *"If it's truth, it must come from God."* However, let it ever be stated: Truth is not a philosophy, which itself is a search after truth, but is a person, and that person is the Lord Jesus Christ (Jn. 14:6; 17:17; I Jn. 5:6). The Word of God claims to hold the answer to all of man's spiritual problems, and the Word of God alone does this (II Pet. 1:3).

"But the angel of the LORD said to Elijah the Tishbite, Arise, go up to meet the messengers of the king of Samaria, and say unto them, Is it not because there is not a God in Israel, that you go to inquire of Baal-zebub the god of Ekron?

"Now therefore thus says the LORD, You shall not come down from that bed on which you are gone up, but shall surely die. And Elijah departed" (II Ki. 1:3-4).

The word *therefore*, as given in Verse 4, is emphatic and means *"for this reason"* or *"on this account."* Because Ahaziah had apostatized from God, the Lord sentenced him to die and not recover from the effects of his fall. It is implied that he might have recovered if he had acted otherwise.

When the messengers came back so soon to Ahaziah, he perceived that they could not have been to Ekron and come back in this amount of time. So, he asked them why they had come back so soon.

Ahaziah knew Elijah and all the miracles that this great prophet had seen, yet he would not call him in but would rather send for the heathenistic gods.

Jesus Christ and Him crucified is the answer for man's dilemma, and the only answer. But the trouble is, the modern church little believes in the Cross; therefore, it resorts to humanistic psychology.

MOAB

"Then Moab rebelled against Israel after the death of Ahab" (II Ki. 1:1).

The word *then* indicates the book is a continuation of I Kings. The two books were one up to the time of the Septuagint translators in the third century B.C. It was then that the book of Kings was divided into two sections.

As stated, Moab had been subdued by David (II Sam. 8:2; 23:20), and after the division of the kingdom, it passed to the Ten Tribe kingdom.

The Moabite stone discovered in 1868 at Dibon in Moab is revealing. The writing is in ancient Hebrew characters down to the time of 140 B.C., when it was replaced by modern square characters in use today.

According to the Moabite stone, Mesha, son of Chemosh-Melech, king of Moab of Dibon, saw his desire upon his enemies after Omri and Ahab had oppressed them for many days. It tells of his victories at Ataroth, Kerioth, Nebo, Jahaz, and other places, and gives all credit to Chemosh, national god of Moab, for past defeats and slavery to Israel because he was angry. He then gives the god credit for victories won after this.

SEEKING HELP FROM DEMON SPIRITS

"And Ahaziah fell down through a lattice in his upper chamber that was in Samaria, and was sick: and he sent messengers, and said unto them, Go, enquire of Baal-zebub the god of Ekron whether I shall recover of this disease" (II Ki. 1:2).

Verse 3 says, *"But the angel of the LORD said to Elijah."* The question was to be addressed to Ahaziah, *"Is it not because there is not a God in Israel, that you go to inquire of Baal-zebub?"*

The Jews changed the name to Beelzebub, *"lord of the dunghill"* (Mat. 12:24). This god is the prince of idols and idolatry, the worst and chief of all wickedness.

ANYTHING OTHER THAN THE CROSS

The church looks askance at the world, even as it should, because it resorts to witchcraft, fortune-telling, and all manner of witchcraft; however, let the following be understood: if the believer's faith is in anything other than the Cross of Christ for whatever reason or problem, in one way or the other, the believer is functioning in witchcraft, i.e., demon spirits.

This means that all believers who resort to humanistic psychology are functioning in the realm of demon spirits. Humanistic psychology, as stated, is not a true science. In fact, it is not a science at all. As someone has well said, and as we have previously stated, its treatment methods are of no value, to say the least. Yet, most of the modern church has opted for this nefarious system. Let us say it again: Humanistic psychology has its roots in atheism, evolution, and humanism, and, in fact, is the religion of humanism. All of this means that its originator is Satan himself, and it is nurtured and fostered by demon spirits.

APOSTASY

As well, every doctrine perpetrated by the church that is not based strictly on the Cross of Christ is in some way spurious.

Concerning these things, Paul said: *"Now the Spirit* (Holy Spirit) *speaks expressly* (pointedly), *that in the latter times* (the times in which we now live, the last of the last days, which begin the fulfillment of end-time prophecies) *some shall depart from the faith* (anytime Paul uses the term 'the faith,' in short, he is referring to the Cross; so, we are told here that some will depart from the Cross as the means of salvation and victory), *giving heed to seducing spirits* (evil spirits, i.e., 'religious spirits,' making something seem like what it isn't), *and doctrines of devils* (should have been translated, 'doctrines of demons'; the 'seducing spirits' entice believers away from the true faith, causing them to believe 'doctrines inspired by demon spirits')" (I Tim. 4:1).

In short, if it's not the Cross of Christ, and we mean the Cross of Christ exclusively, then it's not the gospel, meaning that whatever it is, and no matter how good it may seem to be, it is, in fact, a *"doctrine of demons."*

If that is the case, and most definitely it is, then the modern church is functioning little better, if any at all, than Ahaziah who inquired of Baal-zebub.

ELIJAH THE TISHBITE

Elijah now came on the scene because *"the angel of the LORD"* had spoken to the prophet, telling him what Ahaziah was doing. Actually, the angel of the Lord was most probably a preincarnate appearance of the Lord Jesus Christ.

The king's consultation of Baal-zebub, god of Ekron, was a complete and absolute denial of the divinity of Jehovah. Pulpit says: *"To consult a foreign oracle is equivalent to saying that the voice of God is wholly silent in one's own land. In fact, this was going further into apostasy than Ahab had gone."*

The pronouncement of Elijah to the messenger concerning Ahaziah was straight and to the point: *"Thus says the LORD, You shall not come down from that bed on which you are gone up, but shall surely die"* (II Ki. 1:4).

YOU SHALL SURELY DIE!

Bringing this up to modern times, if the truth be known, many so-called believers, or else, those who were once truly believers but have compromised their way, die before their time because of apostasy. While this definitely doesn't apply to all who die prematurely, it most definitely does, I think, apply to many, if not most.

Listen again to Paul: *"Wherefore whosoever shall eat this bread, and drink this cup of the Lord, unworthily* (tells us emphatically that this can be done, and is done constantly, I'm afraid), *shall be guilty of the body and blood of the Lord* (in danger of judgment, subject to judgment).

"But let a man examine himself (examine his faith as to what is its real object), *and so let him eat of that bread, and drink of that cup* (after careful examination).

"For he who eats and drinks unworthily, eats and drinks damnation to himself (does not necessarily mean the loss of one's soul, but rather temporal penalties, which can become much more serious), *not discerning the Lord's body.* (Not properly discerning the Cross refers to a lack of understanding regarding the Cross. All of this tells us that every single thing we have from the Lord comes to us exclusively by means of the Cross of Christ. If we do not understand that, we are not properly 'discerning the Lord's body.')

"For this cause (not properly discerning the Lord's body) *many* (a considerable number) *are weak and sickly among you* (the cause of much sickness among Chris-

tians), *and many sleep.* (This means that many Christians die prematurely. They don't lose their souls, but they do cut their lives short. This shows us, I seriously think, how important properly understanding the Cross actually is.)" (I Cor. 11:27-30).

I think it should be understood that the Lord does not at all look kindly upon the believer straying from the plainly revealed Word of God, i.e., the Cross of Christ. As death was pronounced upon Ahaziah, likewise, physical death continues to be pronounced upon some, and most definitely spiritual death is pronounced upon all apostasy.

WHAT IS APOSTASY?

Pure and simple, it is a departure from truth.

What is truth?

First of all, let's see what it isn't! Truth isn't a philosophy, which, in itself, is a search for truth. Actually, truth is the following:

- Jesus Christ is truth: He said, *"I am the way, the truth, and the life"* (Jn. 14:6).
- The Word of God is truth: Jesus said, *"Sanctify them through Your truth: Your Word is truth"* (Jn. 17:17).
- The Holy Spirit is truth: John the Beloved wrote, *"And it is the Spirit who bears witness, because the Spirit is truth"* (I Jn. 5:6).

In all of this, truth can be summed up in Jesus Christ and what He did at the Cross. That is the *"Word"* of God (Jn. 1:1), which is all superintended by the Spirit (Jn. 16:3-15).

ELIJAH

"And he said unto them, What manner of man was he which came up to meet you, and told you these words?

"And they answered him, He was an hairy man, and girt with a girdle of leather about his loins. And he said, It is Elijah the Tishbite.

"Then the king sent unto him a captain of fifty with his fifty. And he went up to him: and, behold, he (Elijah) *sat on the top of an hill. And he spoke unto him, You man of God, the king has said, Come down"* (II Ki. 1:7-9).

Elijah, within himself, had no power to do good or harm. He could but pray to the Lord, and in the Lord's wisdom and perfect goodness, He could either grant or refuse the petition. God's answer in sending the fire was His response to Ahaziah and those who served him.

If men do not trust the Lord and what He has done to redeem humanity, and I speak of Christ and the Cross, then, ultimately, the fire of judgment will fall upon them. It is inevitable!

Due to the fact that the Lord sent Elijah to Ahaziah, if the king had truly repented, it seems that even at this late date, the sentence of death could have been altered; however, there was no repentance!

Because Ahaziah had no son, he was succeeded by his younger brother Jehoram. This meant that both kings of Israel and Judah at this time were named *Jehoram*.

THE JUDGMENT OF GOD

"And Elijah answered and said to the captain of fifty, If I be a man of God, then let fire come down from heaven, and consume you and your fifty. And there came down fire from heaven, and consumed him and his fifty" (II Ki. 1:10).

Verses 9 through 16 of II Kings, Chapter 1, portray to the seeking reader that which God demands of those who would come to Him. Too many approach God with the same arrogant demands as the first two captains, whom Ahaziah sent after Elijah. Each had 50 soldiers with him. The Scripture says in Verse 12, *"And the fire of God came down from heaven, and consumed him and his fifty."*

Tragically, much of the modern church has lost its fear of God, and because the church has lost, or is losing, its fear of God, the nation as a whole is following suit. His name is constantly blasphemed publicly over television. His Word is being flaunted with disrespect in every capacity. The nation as a whole is beginning to sanction same-sex marriages, which are an abomination in the eyes of God, and tragically so. Please understand, God's answer to homosexuality when it was flaunted in His face — meaning that those in such bondage would not repent — was the destruction of Sodom and Gomorrah. To be sure, God tolerates this sin now no less than He did then, and even less. While He is opposed to all sin in every capacity, as should be obvious, still, some sins are worse than others, and homosexuality is one of the very worst, if not the very worst.

JUDGMENT

Judgment is also waiting in the wings as it regards the terrible sin of abortion that has taken the lives of untold millions of babies and has stained this nation with blood. Now we are adding the abomination of homosexuality to the list.

These statements are not meant to lambaste the homosexual as an individual. I am not opposed to homosexuals; I am opposed to homosexuality. I am not opposed to alcoholics; I am opposed to alcoholism. I'm not opposed to gamblers; I am opposed to gambling. I'm not opposed to drug addicts; I am opposed to drug addiction. To be opposed to a person because of what he is, in effect, means that one must be opposed to the entirety of mankind, and even oneself. There are no perfect people! Our Lord's motif was to love the sinner and hate the sin, and that must be our motif as well! I love the Muslim, and I mean that sincerely, but I hate the religion of Islam because I know what it does to people.

One does not have to be opposed to people to oppose sin. In fact, one cannot scripturally oppose sin, at least correctly, unless he loves the sinner. The Scripture still says, *"While we were yet sinners, Christ died for us"* (Rom. 5:8).

However, true love, exactly as does the Word of God, will tell the truth. Sometimes the truth is not pleasant to hear, nevertheless, it still must be related exactly as it is.

To tell the homosexual that everything is fine with him is not helping him. The same would go for the alcoholic, the Muslim, and anything or anyone else for that matter.

WAS THE LORD CRUEL FOR SENDING FIRE FROM HEAVEN ON THESE MEN?

No!

More than likely, King Ahaziah, in sending 50 men with a captain to the top of the hill to take Elijah by force, intended to kill him. He had not liked the message sent by Elijah concerning his appealing to Baal-zebub for healing, so he would stop the voice that had called him to task.

As well, Baal was supposed to be the god of the elements, which included fire; so, the Lord would show the king of Israel who was the real God of fire and, in effect, everything else.

The terminology used by these captains, who experienced the judgment of God when they approached Elijah, seems to have been one of arrogance. They would find that it would not be a profitable day for them.

When the last captain approached Elijah, knowing what had happened to the other two captains, he approached the great prophet with an entirely different attitude. First, he *"fell on his knees before Elijah, and besought him, and said unto him, O man of God, I pray you, let my life, and the life of these fifty your servants, be precious in your sight"* (II Ki. 1:13).

The Lord responded with mercy and grace to this captain, even as the captain had responded to Him in humility.

THE ANGEL OF THE LORD

In answer to the request of this third captain, the Bible says that *"the angel of the LORD said unto Elijah ... "* (II Ki. 1:15).

Whether the angel actually appeared to him, we aren't told. At any rate, he did speak to him and gave directions as to what should be done. As well, this was more than likely a preincarnate appearance of the Lord Jesus Christ.

The manner in which the message was given to this wicked Ahaziah tells us that if he had repented, even at this late date, the Lord would have healed him and, thereby, spared him. But, despite all the miracles performed, even with fire coming down from heaven, and despite the great prophet of God standing before him, actually sent by the Lord, still, he would not repent.

Why is man so stubborn? Why is man so obstinate?

Exactly as Elijah predicted, Ahaziah died, and it was *"according to the Word of the LORD which Elijah had spoken"* (II Ki. 1:17).

"You whose name is called Jesus,
"Risen Lord of life and power,
"O! It is so sweet to trust You,
"Every day and every hour."

"You can keep my feet from falling,
"Even my poor wayward feet;
"You who did present me faultless,
"In Your righteousness complete."

"All the sin in me, my Saviour,
"You can conquer and subdue;
"With Your sanctifying power
"Permeate my spirit through."

"You can keep me upward looking,
"Ever upward in Your face;
"You can make me stand upholden
"By the greatness of Your grace."

"O! What joy to trust You, Jesus,
"Mighty victor o'er the grave,
"And to learn amid earth's shadows
"Your unceasing power to save!"

"Make my life a bright outshining
"Of Your life, that all may see
"Your own resurrection power
"Mightily put forth in me."

ELIJAH
THE TISHBITE

CHAPTER

9

TRANSLATION

CHAPTER NINE

TRANSLATION

"AND IT CAME to pass, when the LORD would take up Elijah into heaven by a whirlwind, that Elijah went with Elisha from Gilgal" (II Ki. 2:1).

Elisha, since called of God, had now been with Elijah for approximately 10 years. His training had been by firsthand observation. It most definitely would prove to be sufficient, which would result in a tremendous visitation for Israel.

Elisha knew that Elijah was about to be taken, but at this stage, not how he would be taken; consequently, he would not let the great prophet out of his sight.

THE PERSISTENCE OF ELISHA

There is a tremendous lesson to be learned here as it regards the last days of the great Prophet Elijah, and the persistence that Elisha evidenced as it regards that which he desired. We must take note of that persistence.

It is the persistent soul who reaps the benefits of what Christ has done for us at Calvary, and only the persistent soul (Lk. 11:5-13).

The things of God are not come by easily. We cannot merit them, and neither can we earn them. They are freely given. Yet, the Lord does not hand out His gifts indiscriminately. In other words, they aren't easily possessed.

We must know and understand that whatever it is that we've received from God, and I mean whatever, is received by grace.

What do we mean by receiving by grace?

THE GRACE OF GOD

The grace of God is simply the goodness of God extended to undeserving saints. In a sense, that could be said of the entirety of mankind. In fact, God can deal with mankind only from the premise of grace for the simple reason that if we had to earn it or merit it, we would be found woefully wanting.

We must understand that grace is made possible entirely by the Cross of Christ. In other words, our Lord is the source of grace, while the Cross is the means by which this great grace is given unto us.

God did not have any less grace 3,000 years ago than He does now. It's the Cross that has made grace available to us and it's the Cross alone. That's what we mean when we say the following:

- Jesus Christ is the source of all things we receive from God.

- The Cross of Christ is the means, and the only means, by which these things can be given to us.
- With that being the case, the Cross of Christ must ever be the object of our faith. In fact, the entirety of the story of the Bible is *"Jesus Christ and Him crucified."* So, when one has his faith in Christ and the Cross, that is having his faith in the Word.
- With this being done, understanding that Christ is the source, and the Cross is the means, and having our faith anchored in Christ and the Cross, the Holy Spirit, who works exclusively within the parameters, so to speak, of the finished work of Christ, will then work mightily on our behalf. He doesn't require much of us, but He does require one thing, and on that He will not bend, and that is that our faith be exclusively in Christ and what He did for us at the Cross (Rom. 6:1-14; 8:1-11; I Cor. 1:17, 18, 23; 2:2; Gal. 6:14; Col. 2:10-15; Phil. 3:17-19).

THE SPIRIT OF TRUTH

"Howbeit when He, the Spirit of truth, is come (which He did on the Day of Pentecost), *He will guide you into all truth* (if our faith is properly placed in Christ and the Cross, the Holy Spirit can then bring forth truth to us; He doesn't guide into some truth, but rather 'all truth'): *for He shall not speak of Himself* (tells us not only what He does, but whom He represents); *but whatsoever He shall hear, that shall He speak* (doesn't refer to lack of knowledge, for the Holy Spirit

is God and knows everything, but rather He will proclaim the work of Christ only): *and He will show you things to come* (pertains to the new covenant, which would shortly be given).

"*He shall glorify Me* (will portray Christ and what Christ did at the Cross for dying humanity): *for He shall receive of Mine* (the benefits of the Cross), *and shall show it unto you* (which He did when He gave these great truths to the Apostle Paul [Rom., Chpts. 6-8; Gal. 1:12]).

"*All things that the Father has are Mine* (has always been the case; however, due to the Cross, all these things can now be given to the believer as well): *therefore said I, that He shall take of Mine, and shall show it unto you* (the foundation of all the Holy Spirit reveals to the church is what Christ did at the Cross [Col. 2:10-15])" (Jn. 16:13-15).

As we shall see, the various places named in this scenario hold a lesson for us as it regards the persistence of Elisha.

GILGAL

They began this odyssey at a place called Gilgal. It has been argued as to whether this was the Gilgal next to Jericho — where the children of Israel under Joshua came into the Promised Land approximately 700 years before — or another Gilgal up north. Scholars have debated it both ways. However, from investigation, I personally think it was the Gilgal up north instead of the one near Jericho. The reason is this: When the two prophets left Gilgal, they went to Beth-el, which is immediately south of Gilgal up north, and then to Jericho. If they had gone first of all to the Gilgal near Jericho, they would then have had to travel quite a ways north to go to Beth-el and then back down to Jericho, which does not seem to make sense.

At any rate, and as previously stated, Gilgal was the beginning for Elisha in the sense of him taking the role of the prophet for the northern kingdom of Israel.

Some of you reading these words are presently standing, spiritually speaking, at your Gilgal. Irrespective of the past, it can be, and, in fact, the Lord intends for it to be, your beginning. You see, the Lord does not function from a "three strikes and you're out" syndrome, but He is ready and willing — irrespective of the past — to make this here and now your beginning, if you will only believe Him, trust Him, and consecrate wholly to Him.

BETH-EL

The word *Beth-el* means *"house of God"*; so, Elijah and Elisha came from the place of beginning, at least for the role that Elisha would play, to the house of God, which was quite a proper place to go.

And yet, all of this is symbolism, but I personally feel it spoke volumes to Elisha. Wherever Elijah went at this time, no doubt, was ordered by the Lord, and all for the benefit, it seems, of Elisha.

Beth-el was the place where Jacob had his encounter with the Lord, as it regarded the ladder to heaven, right after he left home because of problems concerning Esau. So now, as it refers to Elisha, it would in some way speak to him as well!

JERICHO

Jericho was the first obstacle encountered by the children of Israel when they came into the Promised Land after crossing the Jordan. It was one of the greatest cities in the land of Canaan. However, its walls would fall beneath the power of God, and the city would be taken with virtually no casualties whatsoever as it regarded God's people. What had been so formidable now became a symbol of great victory. Once again, this symbolism, I am sure, was not lost on Elisha.

We begin at Gilgal, the place of beginnings, which actually means *"rolled away."*

Elijah then went to Beth-el, meaning the house of God, which is where God once spoke, and I continue to refer to Jacob. Then the two prophets went to Jericho, the scene of the first great victory for the children of Israel so many, many years before, as they would go into the Promised Land. During all of this time, the great prophet was telling Elisha, *"Tarry here."* The answer always was, *"As the LORD lives, and as your soul lives, I will not leave you."*

Undoubtedly, Elisha knew that the days of Elijah were numbered. How much he knew, we aren't told, but there was something there that pressed him — the significance of these last days. Irrespective as to what Elijah told him, at least as it regarded his place and position, he let the great prophet know that he would not leave him, no matter what. This is the persistence that God desired.

So the narrative states, *"And they two went on"* (II Ki. 2:6).

The anointing of the Holy Spirit was upon Elijah. Elisha knew this, so he would not let the great prophet out of his sight.

THE ANOINTING

Let the reader understand the following: The anointing is the key and the criterion for the place and position of the saint of God. Find out who the Lord is anointing with the Holy Spirit and make doubly certain that it, in fact, is the Holy Spirit, and then take up your place beside that person. The anointing is the key!

But, as we have already alluded, there is much fake anointing in the land. However, if the believer will earnestly seek the Lord and ask for leading and guidance, to be sure, he will be led to the right person and the right place.

THE SONS OF THE PROPHETS

"And fifty men of the sons of the prophets went, and stood to view afar off: and they two stood by Jordan" (II Ki. 2:7).

The *"sons of the prophets"* could have had, at least somewhat, the blessing as received by Elisha; however, their thoughts and interests were elsewhere.

While it would not have been proper for the sons of the prophets to have placed themselves in the same position as Elisha, for the Lord had not called them for this purpose, still, they should have been closer than merely to *"view afar off."* This is all too often the condition of the church. At best, it views the anointing from *"afar off."* There is no record in the Scriptures that the sons of the prophets had the anointing; consequently, there is very little good they did in Israel or Judah.

THE CROSSING OF THE JORDAN

This would be the last miracle, it seems, performed by Elijah. Beautifully enough, it would be the first miracle performed by Elisha after the translation of Elijah. Elijah would take his mantle, which was a robe-like affair, smite the Jordan, and the waters would open. He and Elisha would go to the eastern side of the river. This would be at the foot of Mount Pisgah, from where Moses viewed the Promised Land but was not allowed to enter in.

In a sense, Elijah and Elisha were similar to Moses and Joshua; consequently, the Lord would translate Elijah very near where He personally conducted the funeral for Moses. Only Elisha saw the translation of Elijah, and, in fact, no one saw the death and burial of Moses except God.

As the Jordan opened, the Scripture says, *"They two went over on dry ground"* (II Ki. 2:8).

THE DOUBLE PORTION

"And it came to pass, when they were gone over, that Elijah said unto Elisha, Ask what I shall do for you, before

I be taken away from you. And Elisha said, I pray you, let a double portion of your spirit be upon me" (II Ki. 2:9).

Verse 9 proclaims Elijah requesting of Elisha, *"Ask what I shall do for you, before I be taken away from you."*

Quite a statement! That statement, in fact, is asked of the whole church. The answer in the last few years has been very revealing: Money, fame, prestige, influence, recognition, approval, dominion, and more. Precious few have answered as Elisha, *"Let a double portion of your spirit be upon me."* Actually, Elisha was asking for the portion of the firstborn. Elijah responded, *"You have asked a hard thing"* (II Ki. 2:10). It could have been translated, and did actually mean, *"You have staked a great claim."* The request expresses the greatness of the appetite of the heart of Elisha for spiritual power. In other words, Elijah's response was an approval of Elisha's request. He would then continue in this spirit in which Elisha had been functioning from the very beginning, *"If you see me,"* speaking of Elijah's coming translation. Elisha's faith that had remained so very close thus far would have little difficulty in the remainder of the distance.

THE TRANSLATION OF ELIJAH

"And it came to pass, as they still went on, and talked, that, behold, there appeared a chariot of fire, and horses of fire, and parted them both asunder; and Elijah went up by a whirlwind into heaven" (II Ki. 2:11).

In the original Hebrew, it says, *"And Elijah went up in a storm into the heavens."* There is no mention of a whirlwind, for only two of the seed of Adam, Enoch and Elijah, have passed from earth without dying.

Elijah and Elisha were on the eastern side of the Jordan River, with that body of water having just opened miraculously at the behest of the great prophet. Elijah and Elisha were conversing at this time, about what, we aren't told.

All of a sudden, it happened.

That which was invisible to the naked eye became visible to Elisha. He literally saw a chariot of fire and horses of fire. In fact, this progression *"parted them both asunder."*

The word *fire* in the Hebrew, as here used, is *esh* and means *"that which is literal or figurative."* In this instance, it is used in the figurative sense. In other words, the chariot and the horses looked like fire. As should be understood, these were spirit horses, which were actually pulling a chariot.

Some claim that Elijah really did not go up into heaven in the chariot, but rather followed. However, the implication is the opposite; the Lord took the great prophet home to glory in a chariot of fire.

HEAVEN

When Jesus died on the Cross, He paid the terrible sin debt that man owed but could not pay. However, before the Cross, when believers died, they were not taken to heaven, but rather down into paradise, which, in fact, was next door to hell. This was due to the fact that the blood of bulls and goats could not take away sins. Jesus said that there was a *"great gulf"* which separated paradise (Abraham's bosom) from hell itself (Lk. 16:26).

So, where did Elijah go when he was translated? Was it up to heaven, as it regards the abode of God, or down into paradise? Every evidence is that he was taken directly to heaven without going to paradise.

Approximately 900 years later, both Moses and Elijah appeared on the Mount of Transfiguration and conversed with our Lord. In fact, they were seen by Peter, James, and John, who had accompanied the Lord to the top of the mountain. Jesus was there transfigured before them, which means that a light, actually, a living light, so to speak, literally emanated from His person. It was not on Him, but rather from Him, which portrayed who and what He actually was, which was and is deity, despite His human frame, i.e., the incarnation (Lk. 9:28-31).

THE CROSS

Actually, our Lord, Moses, and Elijah *"spoke of His decease which He should accomplish at Jerusalem"* (Lk. 9:31).

In essence, the Cross was the topic of their conversation on the Mount of Transfiguration, which means that this was the topic of conversation in heaven as well!

If it was the topic of conversation then, before the fact, how much should it be the topic of conversation now, considering it is after the fact? I think the answer is obvious!

Moses was a type of the law, thereby, when he died, he went to paradise, which was in the heart of the earth (Lk. 16:19-31).

Elijah was a type of the new covenant under Christ and, thereby, a type of the rapture. When he was translated, he was taken to heaven, the abode of God, and not paradise in the heart of the earth.

Incidentally, Elijah will yet come back to this earth and will preach the gospel, and will do so as the prophet he was and is.

ELIJAH WILL COME BACK

This will take place at about the midpoint of the great tribulation (Mat. 24:21). At that time, both Elijah and Enoch will be brought back because they are the only two human beings who will actually have never died, other than the believers who will go in the rapture when that event takes places. They will minister for approximately three and a half years and will be a sore thorn in the side of the Antichrist. No doubt, their ministry will turn many in Israel to Christ, and possibly the entirety of the world. While the Antichrist will repeatedly try to kill them during that three and a half years, he will not be successful until the very end of that period, when the Lord will allow these two great prophets to then be killed.

Malachi, the last great prophet before John the Baptist, stated, *"Behold, I will send you Elijah the prophet before the coming of the great and dreadful day of the* LORD*"* (Mal. 4:5).

THAT WHICH IS COMING

The following are the notes from The Expositor's Study Bible regarding Malachi 4:5:

"The phrase, *'Behold, I will send you Elijah the prophet,'* does not refer to the coming of John the Baptist, who only came in the spirit of Elijah. It actually refers to *'Elijah the prophet,'* who was translated about 500 years before the time of Malachi, and who will be sent back to the earth by the Lord in the midst of the coming great tribulation.

At that time, he and Enoch of Revelation 11:3 will be used of God mightily as they prophesy in Jerusalem. Their ministry will last for the entirety of the last three and a half years of the great tribulation. Both will be killed by the Antichrist at the end of the great tribulation, *'when they shall have finished their testimony.'* However, after three and a half days, they will be resurrected and raptured (Rev. 11:11-12).

As John the Baptist prepared the way for the first advent of Christ, these two, Elijah and Enoch, will prepare the way for the second coming of Christ.

The phrase, *'Before the coming of the great and dreadful day of the LORD,'* addresses the coming great tribulation, and, more specifically, the second coming. It will be a *'great day'* for God's people and a *'dreadful day'* for His enemies!"

Malachi went on to say, *"And he shall turn the heart of the fathers to the children, and the heart of the children to their fathers, lest I come and smite the earth with a curse"* (Mal. 4:5-6).

"The fathers" speak of the patriarchs and prophets of old.

THE CURSE

The phrase, *"Lest I come and smite the earth with a curse,"* proclaims the obvious fact that there is no word following *"curse"* in the last verse of the old covenant, meaning there is more to follow. Thank God!

In contrast, the word *amen* follows the last words of the book of Revelation, closing the canon of Scripture, because after *"grace,"* which is the theme of the ministry of Christ, there is nothing left to be said but *"amen."* Thank God! The world was not left with a curse, but Jesus Christ came and *"redeemed us from the curse of the law, being made a curse for us"* (Gal. 3:13; Mal. 4:6).

Some claim that Enoch will not be the second witness of Revelation, Chapter 11. They claim the second witness will be Moses because he appeared with Elijah on the Mount of Transfiguration.

While that is possible, we must allow the Scripture to be the final word.

The Scripture says, *"And as it is appointed unto men once to die* (due to the fall, all men are under the sentence of death, and, in fact, all have died spiritually, which means to be separated from God), *but after this the judgment* (the answer to the spiritual death of man is Christ and what He did at the Cross; if Christ the Saviour is rejected, all will face Christ the judge; for as death was inevitable, the judgment is inevitable as well)" (Heb. 9:27).

This pertains to all of humanity, with the exception of those who will go in the rapture (I Thess. 4:13-18).

The only two men on earth who have never died are Enoch and Elijah because they were translated; however, to fulfill this passage, both will come back and minister in Jerusalem, as stated, in the latter half of the great tribulation, which, at the conclusion of that time frame, they shall be killed. This will satisfy the Scripture.

Thus writes the chapter of the ministry and translation of Elijah; however, it definitely is not the last chapter. That will come, as stated, at the latter half of the great tribulation, and then there will be a final chapter of Elijah with all the redeemed and with the Lord Jesus Christ, which chapter will never end.

"All the way my Saviour leads me,
"What have I to ask beside?
"Can I doubt His tender mercy,
"Who through life has been my guide?
"Heavenly peace, divinest comfort,
"Here by faith in Him to dwell;
"For I know whatever befall me,
"Jesus does all things well,
"For I know whate'er befall me,
"Jesus does all things well."

"All the way my Saviour leads me,
"Cheers each winding path I tread,
"Gives me grace for every trial,
"Feeds me with the living bread,
"Though my weary steps may falter,
"And my soul a-thirst may be,
"Gushing from the rock before me,
"Lo! A spring of joy I see,
"Gushing from the rock before me,
"Lo! A spring of joy I see."

"All the way my Saviour leads me,
"O the fullness of His love,
"Perfect rest to me is promised,
"In my Father's house above,
"When my spirit clothed immortal,
"Wings its flight to realms of day,
"This, my song through endless ages,
"Jesus led me all the way,
"This, my song through endless ages,
"Jesus led me all the way."

BIBLIOGRAPHY

CHAPTER 4

George Williams, *Williams' Complete Bible Commentary*, Grand Rapids, Kregel Publications, 1994, Pg. 196

Ibid.

Ibid.

CHAPTER 6

H.D.M. Spence, *The Pulpit Commentary: I Kings 21:15*, Grand Rapids, Eerdmans Publishing Company, 1978

CHAPTER 8

H.D.M. Spence, *The Pulpit Commentary: I Kings 17:1*, Grand Rapids, Eerdmans Publishing Company, 1978

ABOUT EVANGELIST JIMMY SWAGGART

The Rev. Jimmy Swaggart is a Pentecostal evangelist whose anointed preaching and teaching has drawn multitudes to the Cross of Christ since 1956.

As an author, he has written more than 50 books, commentaries, study guides, and The Expositor's Study Bible, which has sold nearly 2 million copies.

As an award-winning musician and singer, Brother Swaggart has recorded more than 50 gospel albums and sold nearly 16 million recordings worldwide.

For nearly six decades, Brother Swaggart has channeled his preaching and music ministry through multiple media venues including print, radio, television and the Internet.

In 2010, Jimmy Swaggart Ministries launched its own cable channel, SonLife Broadcasting Network, which airs 24 hours a day to a potential viewing audience of more than 1 billion people around the globe.

Brother Swaggart also pastors Family Worship Center in Baton Rouge, Louisiana, the church home and headquarters of Jimmy Swaggart Ministries.

Jimmy Swaggart Ministries materials can be found at **www.jsm.org**.

NOTES

NOTES

NOTES

NOTES

NOTES

NOTES

NOTES